Dr Craig Hassed, MBBS, FRACGP, was train[
medicine at Melbourne University and graduate
1984. During that time he had a strong interest
holistic approach to medical education, but there
little to satisfy this interest. There was little inp[
that time from important humanities topics suc
philosophy, ethics, sociology, mind–body medi[
psychology and theological issues. These interests led
to a focus on wellbeing rather than simply treating
illness, be it mental or physical. His subsequent work
as a doctor led him down a general practice stream
with an emphasis on counselling, mind–body
medicine and meditation. In 1988 Craig decided to
make a contribution to bridging these missing links in
medical education through the Monash University
Department of Community Medicine and General
Practice, where he has been teaching ever since. In
that time, working with others, he has been
instrumental in introducing topics such as stress
management, meditation, mind–body medicine,
holistic and integrative medicine approaches to under
and postgraduate medical education.

New Frontiers in Medicine

The body as the shadow of the soul

Dr Craig Hassed

'The creation of Adam' by Michelangelo.

HILL OF CONTENT
Melbourne

First published in Australia 2000
by Hill of Content Publishing
86 Bourke St, Melbourne 3000

© Copyright Royal Australian College of General Practitioners 2000

Cover design by Deborah Snibson, Modern Art Production Group
Typeset by Linda McLaughlan
Printed by Australian Print Group, Maryborough

National Library of Australia
Cataloguing-In-Publication data

Hassed, Craig.
New frontiers: the body as the shadow of the soul.

ISBN 0 85572 312 2

1. Medicine — History 2. Traditional medicine 3. Mind and body —
Health aspects 4. Holistic medicine 5. Medicine — Philosophy. I Title

610

This book is dedicated to the great traditions of wisdom across cultures and throughout history and to the teachers and writers who have made this wisdom so accessible to us. It is also dedicated to those who express wisdom and compassion in the way they live their lives.

Gratitude is given for the open-mindedness, encouragement and support of Monash University, the RACGP and the people who have helped me in my professional life such as Neil Carson, John Murtagh, Leon Piterman, Lyn Clearihan, Steven Sommer and many others with whom I have worked.

Thanks and encouragement is given to the thoughtful and interested medical students who are our future doctors, without whom a teacher is both uninspired and redundant. Last but not least it is dedicated to parents, Bob and Shirley, and to my wife, Deirdre, for all they have selflessly given over my lifetime.

Contents

Introduction

Life is full of paradoxes. For instance, it is strange that we are enjoying all the benefits of previously undreamed of technological advances and yet for all their promise these advances do not seem to be reflected in terms of human flourishing and happiness. Dark clouds in the form of social disharmony and alienation, drug problems, economic instability and numerous wars are gathering on the horizon. Although our survival should never have been more secure than it is now we are closer than we have ever been to making our species extinct either through self-inflicted ecological disaster or war. But such is the nature of clouds that they do not last forever.

Also strange is the fact that much of what makes us ill is associated with inequity. By this is meant that the 'western' diseases challenging us like heart disease and many cancers are largely those of western lifestyle and over-consumption. On the other hand, diseases in the developing world are largely those of deprivation. As we search for technological and scientific solutions to these health problems we have been unable to implement the simple solution of a more equitable use of food and resources. The scientific solutions, including the much heralded genetic engineering, use one form of intelligence. The less technological solution would be to find a cure for greed and humankind's sometimes predatory instincts but this requires a deep understanding of human nature, an entirely different form of intelligence which one might call wisdom. As history repeats itself perhaps this new age will teach us some old lessons and lead to the invention of a new medical specialty; not nuclear, pharmacological or even nutritional medicine but "Philosophical Medicine."

It is easy to be swept along with the notion that science will be able to solve every problem that humankind faces. Indeed science has made a huge contribution to our lives and health both in terms of quality and longevity (although by far the largest contributions to health and longevity have been made by engineers in the form of sewerage, clean water and housing). But there are questions and dilemmas which science will never be able to answer so where will our answers come from? Science can teach us how to make a gun. A gun can be used to protect people but just as easily a gun can be used as a threat to the innocent. The invention is a matter of science and technology but the use to which it is put is entirely a philosophical and psychological question in the realm of ethics and morality. The following simple statement exemplifies the contrast.

"Our scientific power has outrun our spiritual power. We have guided missiles and misguided men."

Martin Luther King, Jr.

So what sort of knowledge is required to take us forward into a brighter future? Is it a mechanistic knowledge? Is it a reductionist knowledge which looks at ever smaller parts of the jigsaw puzzle in ever-increasing detail? This trend seems to have run hand in hand with the secularisation of science. Is it a holistic form of knowledge that we need? This book will argue for the latter, that is, a holistic form of intelligence which does not ignore physical science but puts it into another perspective and informs its use.

Philosophy is literally the "love of wisdom" from the Greek, 'philo' meaning 'love' and 'sophia' meaning 'wisdom.' Science also means knowledge from the Latin 'scio' - 'to know.' Science has many branches including the physical sciences such as biology, physics and astronomy and less tangible disciplines such as politics and economics. By less tangible is meant that these sciences like political or economic science have to allow more directly for the non-physical part of the human being; mind and emotion. The more subtle the science becomes the less measurable it is. Interestingly, in the medical mind it is only in recent decades that psychology has been 'promoted' to the status of a science.

Science can become so compartmentalised that it is often hard to get scientists from different disciplines to communicate their knowledge to those of other disciplines. They use different languages. As a noted researcher in the field of psychoneuroimmunology, Dr David Felten, once said, scientists "would rather use each other's toothbrushes" than share each other's language. It is therefore one of the most promising developments in modern medicine that researchers from different disciplines are collaborating. The most important collaboration has been between the fields of psychology and the biological sciences. This has given birth to the 'bio-psycho-social approach' and to the 'mother science' of 'mind-body medicine' with her offspring of psycho-neuro-immunology,[i] psycho-cardiology,[ii] psycho-endocrinology[iii] and psycho-oncology.[iv] Indeed, it is more patently true than ever it was before that all things are related to each other. No aspect of our physical, emotional, social or spiritual being is separate from any other. Like the 'web of life' a tug in one place moves everything else with it.

Medical science, because we all fall ill at some stage in our lives, is one science which none of us will completely avoid. It draws on so many other sciences, like biology, physiology, psychology and sociology. As such it has the potential to be the least precise of all sciences and yet, because of this broad base, it has the potential to be the most holistic.

In nearly all of the sciences, even the physical ones in which we put so much faith today, it is obvious that what we call knowledge today will almost surely be discarded tomorrow as a bare approximation of the truth at best and, at worst, pure fiction. There are innumerable historical precedents illustrating this. Time and again we bend our thinking and observation to fit with the predominant theory of the day. Galileo had to work long and hard to replace the commonly held but incorrect view of the solar system which put the Earth at the centre instead of the sun. As is known he drew the wrath of the orthodoxy of his day and was made to recant for many years until his ideas were eventually embraced. Even though he was on the right track there have been countless modifications to Galileo's view. The field of quantum physics has challenged our long held views about physical matter. It seems that the more closely we look at subatomic particles the less we find. There are no 'little balls' held together in the nucleus with even smaller balls spinning around them at enormous speeds as we were all taught as children. There is no physical matter at all, only fields of energy pulsating, fluxing and exchanging.

The instability of scientific knowledge I can also remember from my own medical education. A celebrated cardiologist began the first of his series of lectures on clinical cardiology to the knowledge-thirsty medical students. Admittedly, the greatest motivator for attaining knowledge for most students was the desire to pass exams, not the love of knowledge itself, but that is another story. In any case, he began his lecture recounting all the practices and beliefs which were common in cardiology 50 and 100 years ago. We laughed at the naivete of these doctors of old. He then said in a low and sobering voice, "what do we think that doctors 50 and 100 years from now will say about what I am about to teach you?" To most students this was a humorous diversion before getting onto the 'real stuff' but to me it was the most important thing he said in all his lectures. This, to me, was wisdom. It put medical knowledge in perspective.

Sure enough, the truth of his words are immediately apparent to any doctor as they make their way out into clinical medicine and find that much of what was learned as a medical student is already obsolete.

An episode is also remembered from my secondary school education. This was when the deputy principal told a story at school assembly which went roughly as follows. A man asked his teacher to show him heaven and hell. His teacher agreed and inquired as to which the man would like to see first. The man said he wished to see hell first. He was duly transported to a beautiful mansion set amid the most magnificent and bountiful countryside. Entering the mansion the man was taken to a banquet hall of extraordinary opulence where there was spread out the most sumptuous feast he had ever laid eyes on. He quickly perceived, however, that the room was also filled with the most excruciating misery he had ever seen. Despite this opulence people were crying out piteously, sick with starvation. He wondered why this was so and, taking a closer look, he saw that the people were compelled to eat their food with forks which were four feet long, too long to get the food into their mouths. The man wondered who could have been so cruel as to play such a macabre joke on these poor souls. The man then asked to be taken to heaven. His teacher dutifully took him to an identical mansion set in an identical countryside. On entering he was shown to an identical banquet hall with the same feast laid out that he had seen before. The man quickly saw that the people were also compelled to eat with the same four-foot forks and yet, to his surprise, everyone was healthy, happy and well fed. Wondering why he again looked closely. There was only one difference he could see between heaven and hell. In hell people starved because they could not feed themselves. In heaven all were happy because they fed each other.

The message in the story has a universal message for us. It is just as relevant for the relationships between doctors and patients as it is for relationships between family members and countries. One could also reflect on what it could teach us about our attitude towards the environment.

Take another principle like the ancient Greek adage, "moderation in all things." It implies that there is a balance or measure to everything. Neither too much nor too little is healthy. It is obvious that eating too much or too little makes us ill. Too much or too little sleep is unhealthy. There is nothing wrong with pleasure but too much of what we find pleasant leads to habits, addictions, compulsions and illness. The principle of moderation applies right down to the molecular level. Insufficient vitamins are associated with many illnesses whereas too many are also associated with illnesses of a different sort. Melatonin is a hormone associated with good physical health and peace of mind and too little is associated with poor immune function and has negative implications for cancer. The idea that one can't have too much of a good thing leads some to advocate large doses of melatonin but unfortunately, at high doses, melatonin actually has negative effects. Taking from the land in the form of agriculture can be a sustainable process if it is in balance with what is put back. If, however, we try to draw too much out this can only be accommodated for a time. Soon it leads to land degradation, salinity and many other problems. Moderation in all things is a rule for life in whatever we do. Perhaps there are exceptions to the rule, for example, one cannot love too much, if the love is true that is. So perhaps moderation in all things is a rule for the physical world and if we avoid the principle we often find ourselves trying to find ways in which we can avoid the natural consequences of our excesses. This only seems to forestall the inevitable or replace one form of harm with another. Moderation in all things, or finding the balance or measure in any activity, is an example of practical, not theoretical, wisdom.

These examples above illustrate a number of things. They illustrate the limited and changing nature of much of what we call scientific knowledge in which we put an inordinate amount of faith. Such knowledge dates quickly, only ever partially deals with a problem and often has many in-built contradictions. Admittedly much of what passes for wisdom can also be superstition in another disguise. These examples also illustrate the more universal nature of real wisdom in which, unfortunately, we often put so little faith. Such wisdom we experience intuitively.

"Intuition is a sacred gift.
Rationality its faithful servant."

Albert Einstein

True knowledge, that is, knowledge which is actually true, does not change. It encompasses the largest perspective, applies to an infinitely wide range of situations and has no internal contradictions. Contradictions are more the product of our own ignorance, not a lack of intelligence in the universe itself.

This broadest, universal view is the knowledge which philosophy pursues. It does not know temporal or cultural boundaries so it is as relevant for us today as it was for those who lived long ago. The path to wisdom is often a rocky one with many wrong turns down the byways of incorrect opinion, dogma and fixed belief. What is most intriguing and exciting, however, is the potential of combining just a 'spoonful of wisdom' with our scientific knowledge. It seems to help 'the medicine go down' far more smoothly and effectively. As you will read later, there are numerous examples of scientists who manage to combine wisdom with clinical medicine very successfully. New frontiers open up when we reconnect bodies, minds and consciousness. Many possibilities present themselves when we work with natural processes in a more conscious way. The resultant medicine is at the same time far more humane, potent and economical. At the same time it has less of the unwanted side-effects which we so often try to avoid.

It is possible that what we lack today in our modern practice of medicine is this larger view. We sometimes get distracted by detail and miss the principles or laws which underpin the detailed observations we make. Science of the highest order, however, works from principle to the detail and can be just as valid a form of wisdom as philosophical reflection. Great scientists like Einstein or Oppenheimer who heralded in this new age of discovery were every bit as much philosophers as they were physicists.

> *"The general notions about human understanding which are illustrated by discoveries in atomic physics are not in the nature of things wholly unfamiliar, wholly unheard of, or new. Even in our own culture they have a history, and in Buddhist and Hindu thought a more considerable and central place. What we shall find is an exemplification, an encouragement, and a refinement of old wisdom."*
>
> Julius Oppenheimer

Similarly with the founders of modern medicine from the time of Hippocrates and his contemporaries. They often observed and understood phenomena years before the research could be done. The connections between the mind, emotions and bodily defenses were known well before psycho-neuro-immunology was a scientific mature discipline.

> *"The mind in addition to medicine has powers to turn the immune system around."*
>
> Jonas Salk

Science in general and medical science in particular are intensely practical disciplines. They work from practical observations to try and deal with practical issues of daily life. As such they can improve our lives enormously but without humanity and wisdom to guide them scientific knowledge can be easily used wastefully or to the detriment of the humanity it was meant to serve.

Philosophy too can be misguided. The philosopher's flights of fancy can become abstracted so far from the practicalities of worldly affairs and simple experience that they have little real relevance and application to daily life. Hence the philosopher is often accused of being an irrelevant navel gazer. There have also been numerous occasions where philosophy in the form of sophistry has been an artful apologist for many a suspect policy. Philosophy needs to be both practical and benevolent. What use is there for impractical philosophy. Sincere and astute observation of the world leads to wisdom and wisdom guides our lives and actions in the world. The proof of our understanding is always in the pudding. We can fool ourselves but not nature.

This book is a compilation of articles from the 'Philosophy of Medicine' series published in Australia's leading general practice journal, the *Australian Family Physician*. These published articles, together with a few previously unpublished ones, are an attempt to draw together history, philosophical principle and ethics with clinical experience and scientific evidence. It would be overstating things to suggest that at each point this will be successfully and completely achieved but this is the course, I believe, we need to chart. For good reason many in the general public are taking the lead in demanding a more holistic and integrated approach to their medical care. One suspects that the health care system will need to encompass this movement if medicine is to avoid marginalising itself. In this way the medicine of the future may be seen as a return to the past but in a way that is not scientifically naïve. It can encompass philosophical principle and apply it in a contemporary context like never before.

Our technological advances can then be best and most wisely used where first priorities come first and last ones come last and not the other way around. Why do we seem so prepared to treat with a pill or some other surgical or technological solution things which are really the product of thought or western lifestyle? And yet, where indicated we should be ready to make best use of those tremendous advances which medical science has offered us. There is good reason to suggest that we as doctors have been far too ready to reach for the script pad rather than take the time to provide the education, skills and encouragement which the person may need. This dilemma may not be entirely the doing of the profession itself. No group ever functions independently of the community in which it resides. Indeed, the profession may well have come to reflect views which are generally held in the community at large. But if the problems are systemic then the solutions will also be systemic. If the saying "as above so below" is true then change must happen on every level. Far from wishing to get embroiled in politics one could nevertheless use a statement which appears in Plato's classic work, The Republic. He exhorts the need for wisdom to join with political power when he says;

> *"Until philosophers are kings, or the kings and*
> *princes of this world have the spirit and power of*
> *philosophy, and political greatness and wisdom*
> *meet in one, and those commoner natures who*
> *pursue either to the exclusion of the other are*
> *compelled to stand aside, cities will never have*
> *rest from their evils — no, nor the human race, as*
> *I believe — and then only will this our State have*
> *a possibility of life and behold the light of day."*

> Plato: The Republic, book 5.

Perhaps we could, with apologies to Plato, make a few changes to suit our purposes here.

> *"Until philosophers are doctors, or the doctors*
> *and nurses of this world have the spirit and power*
> *of philosophy, and medical greatness and wisdom*
> *meet in one, and those commoner natures who*
> *pursue either to the exclusion of the other are*
> *compelled to stand aside, hospitals and medical*
> *practices will never have rest from their evils —*
> *no, nor the human race, as I believe — and then*

only will this our (ideal) medical system have a
possibility of life and behold the light of day."

It is hoped that you will find this series of articles thought
provoking, informative and sometimes challenging. If more
questions than answers arise, if one is more prepared than
before to take a fresh look at contemporary issues whether they
be medical or non-medical, and if one finds the occasional piece
of practical advice in them, then they will have served their
purpose. Each chapter stands by itself and raises its own questions. Taken individually they may be like parts of a jigsaw
puzzle, but taken as a whole they hopefully go some way
towards filling out a picture of medicine which is both wise and
practical. There are undoubtedly many more pieces to be put in
place yet.

Dr Craig Hassed

Knowledge and intuition

Intuition is a sacred gift.
Rationality its faithful servant.

Albert Einstein

Einstein, the genius that he was, must have known something about the pursuit of knowledge. Why would he value intuition so highly and does it have a place in medical science?

We all have ideas about what constitutes knowledge. To the research scientist it means one thing and to the clinician another. For example, an experienced clinician, when acutely attentive to their patients, seems to use a 'sixth sense.' It can't be learned in a book and it never works from habit. This intuition, for want of a better word, often uncannily directs therapy to the specific and individual needs of that particular patient. As clinicians we know this 'sixth sense' exists and yet it is hard to define and describe.

Intuition operates in other ways too. Scientific discoveries are often made intuitively, as in Einstein's case, long before the experiment could be performed. In ethical decisions it may be that 'conscience' conveys a similar meaning to intuition being a form of knowing whose 'proof is in the pudding.' That feeling of unease before taking a wrong course of action may be of more value than we generally ascribe to it. Nevertheless, it is interesting that concepts like intuition and conscience are almost entirely out of use in scientific and ethical discussion these days.

Where does knowledge come from?

This conception of intuitive knowledge is a very old one. Plato and Socrates considered that wisdom or true knowledge were already 'implanted in the soul' and that all learning and education was a matter of drawing out that knowledge. The word education in fact comes from a Latin word 'educare' which means 'to draw out'.[1] Ignorance, on the other hand, is merely 'forgetting'.

> Those who are said to learn only remember, and
> learning is recollection only.
>
> Plato — Phaedo

For this purpose of 'recollection' humankind was given the gift of reason, not in the sense of the often convoluted process of endlessly intellectualising about things and never getting anywhere, but rather reason in the sense of an incisive, quiet and immediate knowing. Far from complicating an issue, reason draws the obvious out of the convoluted, the simple out of the complex, sheds light on what was in the dark, and reveals the law behind the activity. Perhaps we appreciate this when we acknowledge the genius and incredible simplicity in a great insight, invention or discovery. Such intelligence cannot be reproduced artificially. This point seems to me to be represented artistically by Michelangelo in the The Creation of Adam.[2] (*see title page*) Symbolically, God is painted within what is a very accurate anatomical cross section of the human brain with its frontal lobes, pituitary gland, brain stem, cerebellum and corpus callosum represented by God's left arm. The gift of intelligence seems to be awakening and enlivening man.

Intuition and new discoveries

The previous discussion would be of little relevance to us as doctors unless we could find practical examples that change the way we view illness and practice medicine. In medical research there are numerous examples of investigators whose intuition has led them to ground breaking discoveries. The work of Dean Ornish investigating the management of coronary artery disease (CAD) is one case in point. Until his work, it was widely held that this was an irreversible illness. His personal experiences in using a holistic approach to cope with poor health as a medical student kindled in him a deep conviction that such an approach provided the right environment for the body to reverse even advanced and life-threatening illnesses. He took patients with established CAD and randomised them into two groups.[3] The intervention group undertook comprehensive lifestyle change (including stress management, group support, moderate physical exercise, low-fat vegetarian diet and ceasing smoking) along with the usual medical management, except for lipid-lowering drugs, and the control group had the usual medical management. His was the first demonstration that the body could in fact reverse what was previously held to be an irreversible process. It was found that at 1 year the CAD had reversed in 82% of patients. Symptomatically they were also much better and their quality of life was significantly improved compared to the controls. This was compared with 53% of the control group whose CAD had worsened (in fact the only ones to improve had also made significant lifestyle changes of their own accord). There was a strong 'dose response' relationship between lifestyle change and regression of CAD. Two and 5 year follow up has shown that the divergence between the two groups is sustained and increasing.[4-6] Although there is much that we still do not know about the mechanisms of how stress reduction, group support, and lifestyle change work so potently the potential is enormous and the lesson salient. The combination of such intuition, subjected to the rigours of evidence based medicine, is potent. Similar outcome studies for other chronic conditions need to be done.

Interestingly, Ornish's program cost less than one tenth of the more expensive coronary bypass procedure. Perhaps good clinical care, quality of life, health and economics obey the same principles? Despite this, we in Australia have been slow to adopt this comprehensive approach to therapy. One would certainly not wish to forgo the great advances that technology has made but perhaps it is sometimes used at the expense of first principles. Many patients share similar intuitions with clinicians such as Dr Ornish by attributing importance to their holistic well being, stress, emotions and other lifestyle factors at a far greater rate than their doctors.[7]

Are new perspectives needed?

Perhaps we need to review the way we look at knowledge. When we see it as merely a volume of information then we may well miss the obvious, confuse priorities and waste a lot of resources in the process. If knowledge is taken to be an understanding of the universal principles or laws underpinning the phenomena we observe, then perhaps we might approach research and therapy in a different way. There may come a time when we, as scientists and clinicians, give intuition and conscience the respect they deserve.

The body is the shadow of the soul

'The body is the shadow of the soul.'[1]

Marsilio Ficino

To a scientist the mind–body connection is a complicated web of physiological processes of infinite complexity. The more we look the more complex it seems to become. And yet, to a philosopher, it is a simple metaphysical relationship where the complex is governed by simple laws.

Marsilio Ficino (1433–1499) was what you might call a 'meta-physician'. He was the head of the Platonic Academy in renaissance Florence and was known as a philosopher, scholar, physician, musician and priest and was largely responsible for reintroducing Platonic teaching to the West which is significant because at the heart of a renaissance there tends to be a philosophical revival. Frequently, in Western civilisation, it has been a Platonic revival. In many ways Florence was the centre of this flowering of the arts, literature and sciences and Ficino was noted for communicating the philosophy through very beautiful, inspiring and instructive letters to notable people of his day.

The creative intelligence

One simple but potent statement from one of the letters is recorded on the previous page. Ficino uses a metaphor to convey, with great simplicity, concepts that are quite sophisticated, such as the mind–body relationship. Shakespeare, who was also profoundly influenced by Platonic ideas, made use of the same metaphor.

> *'Life's but a walking shadow, a poor player*
> *that struts and frets his hour upon the stage*
> *and then is heard no more.'*[2]

This is no doubt a sobering comment upon our 'worldly existence.' Such statements, however, have a practical as well as a philosophical use. They can be seen as summing up the essence of the ever expanding field of scientific endeavour called mind–body medicine, so let us explore their practical implications for a moment. A shadow needs a source of light, an object to intercept the light and a surface to project the shadow on to. The Platonic view was that the light by which we see things is our consciousness — our 'soul' or 'self'. What the consciousness illuminates is the 'psyche' or mind made up of all its thoughts, emotions and sensations. The result is that these thoughts and emotions, powered by consciousness, produce physical effects. That is, they move the body all the way from the biochemistry and genes, down to the muscles. In simple terms, if one feels an emotion like anger or joy then the body language, behaviour and physiology respond accordingly. If one has a desire for food then the body moves to the fridge or the restaurant. We may not always be aware of our thoughts and emotions, but nevertheless, they have their effects. If one has a desire to create something, and has access to the knowledge and resources to do it, then the thing will physically manifest. Ficino, as did Einstein, believed that this creative intelligence drove the whole of the natural world and not just things we commonly consider 'man made.'[3]

Implications for health

Are there implications for our health and clinical medicine? Exploring the field of metaphysics scientifically is a far greater challenge for the researcher or clinician than just measuring a blood pressure. Trying to distinguish between what is a valid understanding of non-physical processes and what are just fanciful, impractical and nebulous ideas is not easy. Nevertheless, a lot of very fine work has already gone in to researching mind–body themes. Some excellent well referenced and readable reviews of the research are appearing[4] and our understanding of the long term effects of unhealthy stress, which we so commonly experience in association with modern day living, is becoming ever more sophisticated. New scientific terms like 'allostatic load', which is the 'long term effect of the physiologic response to stress', are often old concepts in contemporary language.[5]

New studies are appearing all the time and demonstrating relationships between psychological and social variables which we may not have considered before. For example, a low level of job control, whether self reported or independently assessed, is associated with a nearly doubled risk of coronary heart disease even when controlled for all the other usual risk factors.[6] Elsewhere it has been shown that depression is a risk factor for osteoporosis. Women with depression have considerably lower bone mineral densities and higher cortisol excretions than controls.[7] The more we look the more we find. It is a shame that many studies looking at physical illnesses do not include an arm to assess psychological factors.

Finding the balance

We have to be a little careful in acknowledging the mind as such an important lynchpin in our health. The idea 'it is all in the mind' leads us to forget that it is 'also in the body'. The mind and the body, like the driver and the automobile, are insepa-rable. The temperament of the former affects the condition of the latter. By being too conscious of one we can neglect the other. It is easy to forget to check the thyroid gland of a patient who presents complaining of stress. A balanced approach will always be best. Many doctors and patients perceive modern medicine as having undervalued the role of mind. Hopefully we will find that point of balance rather than the pendulum swinging to extremes.

As a practising doctor it is easy to avoid the patient's thoughts, feelings and social situation as vital parts of their total management plan. For many of us the thought of counselling and psychological interventions conjures up ideas of great time commitment or skills we think we don't have. That having been said, even brief counselling interventions by GPs can have long term psychological benefits, and produce better patient satisfaction and health outcomes.[8,9,10] Even if we don't provide the intervention ourselves, having identified the problem we should have an idea of referral resources around us who can provide the needed support.

In conclusion, modern medicine seems to be turning full circle and returning to its ancient origins. To the ancient Greeks, harmony of mind and body was a central concept in their view of themselves and the cosmos. Body and mind were inseparable and both had to be treated together. Perhaps Plato's words may be as relevant for us today as they were 2500 years ago.

> *'You ought not to attempt to cure the body without the soul. ... For this is the great error of our day in the treatment of the human body, that physicians separate the soul from the body.'*[11]

The rule of nature

*This is a moral universe. Right and wrong do matter.
Our choice in favour of truth and goodness, our
individual acts of courage, honesty, standing up for
the truth do not evaporate into the ether.*

Archbishop Desmond Tutu
London School of Economics, February 1995

The actions and personal commitment of people such as
Archbishop Tutu and Nelson Mandela probably speak far more
loudly than their words. Freedom and morality are two things to
which most individuals, groups and nations aspire. In fact there
cannot really be a notion of morality without the ability to
choose, guided by the agency of reason. We do not consider a
plant, machine, animal or even a young child as responsible
moral agents because they do not have the necessary faculties.

Is morality absolute?

What is the standard by which we gauge actions as either right
or wrong? Whose standard is it and where did it come from? Are
there absolute or only relative moral laws? If we aspire to ideals
like freedom and morality then does our aspiration come from

something innate in us, like conscience, or is it all a matter of utility? Or maybe morality and expediency correspond? Do we only become aware of the importance of freedom and morality when we lack them? To what extent are we really free to choose our morals and ethics? Although such questions may seem abstract they impact on every aspect of health care and ethics. Where do we begin to unravel the question of whether a minor should be given a script for the pill, or whether heroin should be decriminalised, or whether we should prescribe a medication that is contrary to established evidence?

Physical laws of nature

One way of approaching this problem is by defining right and wrong in terms of our willingness to obey natural laws. For example, do we have a choice whether or not to obey the laws of gravity, aerodynamics or mathematics? No! We are bound to obey them whether we wish to or not for they will act regardless of our understanding of them. On this level the laws of nature are non-negotiable. It is obvious that on the physical level, our opinions about such laws have absolutely no effect on them. We cannot, for example, legislate against the law of gravity simply because we find it inconvenient, unpopular or because it abuses our right to fly.

Are there natural laws of morality?

What is far more challenging and contentious is whether such laws exist on levels governing our psychology, behaviour, politics or society. Are there natural laws of morality which we are just as bound to obey as the physical laws? If so, then they must transcend cultural and temporal boundaries, be non-negotiable and the 'fall' associated with ignoring them would be painful and inevitable. If this were so, we as humans would have no 'input' into the law making but rather our written laws would reflect these natural laws. Our collective response to this premise underpins our legislation, social structures, and ethical codes. A shift in thinking on this premise will be reflected in many changes in law and policy in the medical setting.

From a religious perspective

The 'traditional' and essentially religious view has been that the whole of nature is governed by laws decreed by God. This view was the cornerstone of our legal system for centuries. It was intimated in Blackstone's classic introduction to the Common Law of England.

> *When the supreme being formed the universe,*
> *and created matter out of nothing, He impressed*
> *certain principles upon that matter, from which it*
> *can never depart, and without which it would*
> *cease to be. When He put that matter into motion,*
> *He established certain laws of motion, to which all*
> *moveable bodies must conform. And, to descend*
> *from the greatest operations to the smallest, when*
> *a workman forms a clock, or other piece of*
> *mechanism, he establishes at his own pleasure*
> *certain arbitrary laws for its direction.*

Sir William Blackstone —
Commentary on the Laws of England

From this point of view moral precepts are decreed by a 'divine will' that this is the natural order of things, and not because a group of human beings have decided that it is the right thing. Only this divine will has the right to dictate to other human beings.

The natural law is binding for each individual and society. And any consequence such as social or economic hardships are the natural and unavoidable consequences of going against these natural laws. Nature will not be denied although the working out of the law may take years or even generations.

We are only free within the boundaries set by the law and, like any game, playing without adhering to the rules leads to chaos, unhappiness and confusion. Adherence leads to order, happiness and ease. Although all cultures and religions do express their moral codes differently, and principle can easily become buried in dogma, there are nevertheless great similarities between these various traditional religious moral codes.

From a secular perspective

A more modern secular view, especially since the time of Mill, Darwin, Marx, and Freud has tended to turn away from a sense that a divine will is governing both nature and our actions and so we are, as it were, masters of ourselves. There are natural physical laws that we must obey, but social, behavioural, moral and political systems are of our own making according to personal or popular opinion and fashion. Expediency is divorced from morality and thoughts of the universe being permeated by a conscious, intelligent and benevolent force are little more than primitive superstition.

In this view we have far more scope to accommodate personal freedoms and expression in our lives. To Marx, for example, traditional religious laws and precepts were a part of the 'opiate of the masses.' He postulated that they stopped people questioning and thinking for themselves and were a way of manipulating society to conform to the will of often selfish rulers thereby making it easier to handle. Threats of divine retribution for disobeying natural and divine laws were considered a cruel and confabulated threat in order to realise these ambitions. This according to Marx can be seen throughout history as many an abuse of rights has arisen from the rise of social constructs like religion with all its rigidity and dogmatism.

This brings us full circle to the position that moral rules are arbitrary and flexible and so we are entering a brave new world of possibilities in the modern era. Whether this new 'freedom' is a gateway to prosperity or chaos, we shall discover in due course.

Is there another perspective?

Perhaps there are many ways of looking at the issue. Take a moral precept like 'treating your neighbour as yourself.' Maybe it is just as relevant to us all whether one calls oneself spiritual, atheist, humanist, environmentalist or just plain practical. Maybe various moral codes and theories are describing different aspects of the same thing and ascribing different causes to it according to their understanding.

The aim of this discussion is not to promote one view or another but rather to open up the principle for consideration. The above discussion might otherwise seem like a philosophical flight of fancy except for the fact that virtually every decision we make, medical or personal, will be consciously or unconsciously governed by our answers to a few fundamental questions. Each of us must decide for ourselves. So without trying to reach a conclusion here, the questions will be left open. What do you think? What are the laws of nature? Where did they come from? How far do they go? What are the implications for one's life and work?

Spirituality and health

Recently I came across a very interesting review article which had 77 references examining the relationship between religious commitment and mental or physical health.[1] It was clear from the research that an active 'religious commitment' was beneficial for preventing mental and physical illness, improving recovery and enhancing the ability to cope with illness, although different people might define religiosity in different ways. Even when the studies were prospective or retrospective, or when they controlled for other lifestyle and social variables the relationship still held. Some of the notable points included far lower rates of substance abuse, anxiety, depression and suicide. Included in the physical benefits were lower rates of hypertension, heart disease and cancer.[2,3] This is confirmed consistently with new data suggesting findings such as lower substance abuse for adolescents,[4] quicker recovery from depression[5] and reduced hypertension.[6] Despite this there is a general tendency in the medical literature not to take religious issues seriously and to even look on them as a negative influence.

The above raises a lot of interesting and challenging questions for us as clinicians, medicine being a largely secular, scientific discipline. Religion often gets a bad press in medical and psychiatric circles, and sometimes for good reason. For example, a recent article looked at a series of preventable paediatric deaths associated with the parents' religious views preventing or delaying medical attention.[7] Such extreme examples of religion playing a negative role are, thankfully, rare. But they can serve to obscure the positive role it plays in a great many people's lives. Perhaps a reasonable and balanced view accommodates the appropriate use of science and technology with spirituality.

Finding the soul of science

> *'Science without religion is lame, religion without science is blind.'*

> Albert Einstein

Other fields of science, such as physics, may also be rekindling their philosophical and spiritual roots. One of the striking things about reading the words of the great pioneers in science is that they were as much mystics as they were scientists. They thought holistically and broadly. An appreciation of the beauty, order and harmony in the laws of nature inevitably draws the mind to a contemplation of the innate intelligence underpinning them.

> *'Every one who is seriously involved in the pursuit of science becomes convinced that a spirit is manifest in the laws of the universe — a spirit vastly superior to that of man, and one in the face of which we with our modest powers must feel humble. In this way the pursuit of science leads to a religious feeling of a special sort, which is indeed quite different from the religiosity of someone more naive.'*

> Albert Einstein

'Religion' has an interesting etymology coming from the Latin word 'relegare' which means 'to tie together'. It suggests some sort of recognition of the unity and interconnectedness of people and the world. Spirituality and religion, of course, overlap and are often used interchangeably. People define and express spirituality in different ways. Scientists, like Einstein, can express it through the pursuit of knowledge. For most it is associated with formal religion through faith. Philosophers seek it through the use of reason. Some find transcendence and meaning through beauty and artistic expression, while others find it through humanitarian pursuits, and for many today it may be associated with an environmental consciousness. It is also possible for religion to be defined in a narrow and dogmatic way that is potentially a source of division, rigidity and intolerance.

The search for meaning

In any case, the search for meaning through spirituality has been intrinsic to all cultures through all times and is within every human being, though it may lie dormant. As children we were born asking large and unfathomable questions. Have we lost our sense of awe and wonder in the medical and psychological sciences? Do we avoid examining these issues because we find answers hard to come by?

The search for meaning seems to be a universal human need that is all too easily taken for granted in our lives, doctors as well as patients. It is often observed, especially among many adolescents today, that this need can be over-ridden, deflected or suppressed by many things. The costs for our young in terms of depression, anxiety, alienation and substance abuse are becoming apparent even today and the long term costs may be far larger than we envisaged. Idealism is a hard thing to maintain in the modern day but perhaps it is a prerequisite for healing more deeply.

The lack of meaning in life is a soul-sickness
whose full extent and full import our age has not
as yet begun to comprehend.

Carl Jung

So what are some of the issues raised by this discussion? It may be that the intangibles of our lives, which we as scientists find so hard to define and measure, do have a central role in our well being. They may well be an important determining factor in why we get ill, how well we recover, and how well we cope with illness. Perhaps, even if we are not religious ourselves, we still need to ask questions about how our patients find meaning in their lives in a way that is not dogmatic but is respectful of their religious and cultural background. Taking care not to push a line of thought, it may be that medical education needs to sensitively encompass such questions. It may be time that the strength and potential for healing which spirituality offers needs to be consciously tapped as a part of a truly holistic approach to health care.

Western psychology meets Eastern philosophy

A recent trend noted with a mix of enthusiasm and suspicion by many psychiatrists, psychologists, counsellors and doctors is the move away from modern psychological explanations to more holistic and ancient philosophical solutions for the age old problems of stress, depression, anger, grief and relationship breakdown.

One example of a cross pollination between philosophy and psychology, and between East and West, was a recently released book called *The Art of Happiness*.[1] In it, a psychiatrist, Howard Cutler, questions the world leader of Tibetan Buddhism, Nobel Peace Prize winner and statesman, the Dalai Lama. The conversation is a fascinating one. This article will give an overview of some of the main themes considered.

The search for happiness

The search for new ways to deal with old problems may be a timely one. Mental health for the young seems to be declining in most Western countries. In Australia approximately 20%[2] of adults experience a major mental health problem in one year with the highest prevalence rates (27%) occurring in the 18–24 year age group.[2] The long term effects of such a situation are hard to fathom but with the epidemic of depression expected in the next century we may have to do some serious soul searching quite soon.

Although, on the surface, we all seem so different we undoubtedly all want to be happy and free of suffering.

'I believe that the very purpose of our life is to seek happiness. That is clear.'[1]

The Dalai Lama

We tend to be so conscious of the pace and stresses of every day living that we rarely pause to ask some very basic questions about the nature of happiness. Indeed, especially from the time of Freud, most of our modern ideas about psychology are formed from the thinking of those with psychopathology rather than the thinking of those who are noted for being happiest. Put another way, we have followed an illness rather than a wellness model.

The Dalai Lama tends to avoid our modern 'quick fix' mentality, opting instead for a philosophy largely drawn from simple observations and reasoning. However, he does suggest that there are principles that would yield results if patiently and conscientiously followed over time.

One of the starting points in searching for happiness and healthy relationships is acknowledging our essential nature; that is, what is common to all people, rather than what separates us. This underlying commonality or unity is a firm basis for compassion, empathy and understanding, whereas the differences such as colour, nationality, religion and gender are superficial only. When our commonality is forgotten then the differences become a potential source of division and conflict between people.

Happiness versus pleasure

Even if we all want happiness and freedom from suffering we pursue it in different ways. One common notion that seems to have pervaded popular culture, media and advertising, is that happiness equates with pleasure and material possessions.

> *'Now sometimes people confuse happiness with*
> *pleasure. ... True happiness relates more to the*
> *mind and heart. Happiness that depends on*
> *physical pleasure is unstable; one day it's there,*
> *the next day it may not be.'[1]*

The Dalai Lama

The Dalai Lama suggests that the assumption that happiness results from gaining more and more, may be one of the key factors behind greed, overindulgence and acquisitiveness. This over acquisitiveness leads to many problems and seems to preclude cooperation, altruism and understanding while selecting for a predatory and competitive attitude. Overindulgence in the things that are natural and that we find pleasurable, whether it be food, leisure time, sleep or sex can turn them into something negative and result in suffering. Rather than a recipe for happiness and freedom this kind of thinking may be a recipe for addiction, fear, anxiety, anger, grief, depression and many other negative emotional states. Not everything that pleases us is good for us and not everything that is unpleasant is bad for us. The remedy may require a change of attitude by examining some of the assumptions we make. Pleasure and pain are not right or wrong in themselves but give us useful information about the environment and potential harm. Mostly they are transitory and do not seem to provide long term happiness and contentment.

Human nature

Aggression versus compassion

Another crucial issue examined is human nature. Many contemporary theories in psychology and biology hold the view that human nature is essentially aggressive and motivated by self interest which is covered by a veneer of civilisation. The Dalai Lama suggests it is the other way around. Compassion and self-lessness are really central to our nature but are covered by an indoctrinated, conditioned, habituated and unquestioned veneer of aggression and intolerance. Thus one can practice empathy and compassion if one is patient and persistent. How can we know if this compassion is really in keeping with our true nature? He suggests that the ability to be happy and feel at peace with oneself are good indicators. If we are regularly angry, intolerant and predatory we tend to live in fear, anxiety and mistrust of our fellow human beings; not a recipe for contentment. The opposite is true for those who cultivate altruism and compassion.

The role of guilt

As the Dalai Lama is a symbol of wisdom for many in the world, it may be assumed that he would be unacquainted with emotions such as guilt. This is not the case, however he deals with it a little differently.

> *'But even though that feeling of regret is still there,*
> *it isn't associated with a feeling of heaviness or a*
> *quality of pulling me back. It would not be helpful*
> *to anyone if I let that feeling of regret weigh me*
> *down, be simply a source of discouragement and*
> *depression with no purpose, or interfere with*
> *going on with my life to the best of my ability.'*[1]

His advice seems to accord well with both intuition and evidence that suggests that although the tendency to chronic guilt is associated with poor mental health the ability to feel guilt for a wrongdoing or mistake and to learn from it is associated with better mental health.[3] This suggests it may be important to help people discern the difference between appropriate and inappropriate guilt as they warrant different responses.

Finding meaning in suffering

> *'Man is ready and willing to shoulder any*
> *suffering as soon and as long as he can see a*
> *meaning in it.'*

Victor Frankl

While no one would choose to suffer, the realities of life suggest no one can totally avoid suffering in the form of death, loss or illness. What one can consciously choose, however, is one's attitude to the suffering. It can be willingly borne with a conscious examination of it enabling one to find the root cause of the suffering. By such an approach one not only bears the adversity with more equanimity but also comes to an understanding of the ways in which our behaviour contributes to the problems.

> 'Reflecting on suffering has tremendous importance
> because by realising the nature of suffering, you will
> develop greater resolve to put an end to the causes
> of suffering and the unwholesome deeds that lead
> to suffering. And it will increase your enthusiasm
> for engaging in the wholesome actions and deeds
> that lead to happiness and joy.'[1]

In closing

The book had many more themes than can be considered here including finding balance, dealing with negative emotions like anger and hatred, the need for a regular contemplative or meditative practice, dealing with habit, questions as to the nature of self, and attitudes towards death. It is interesting to note that many of the principles suggested by quite ancient philosophical teachings seem to be giving us insights into problems that the Western world sees looming on the horizon. Intuitively many in the general public are turning to deeper philosophical answers for inescapable human dilemmas. At the same time psychologists, counsellors and doctors can use these approaches to good effect and the scientific relationships between emotions, social factors, contemplative practices and health are becoming more clearly elucidated.

The Dalai Lama was at pains to point out that each person and culture needs to look at these issues in a way that is appropriate to them. The problems and solutions may well be universal and therefore are not confined by social or cultural boundaries.

What is orthodox medicine?

The Australian Medical Council (AMC), like other medical councils around the world, is formulating educational guidelines and a policy with respect to 'unorthodox' medicine, which often goes by other names such as 'complementary', 'integrative' or 'alternative' medicine.

Defining orthodox medicine

In order to know what is 'unorthodox' we must first define 'orthodox' medicine. The AMC's proposed dividing line between orthodox and unorthodox is that orthodox is 'scientific' and unorthodox is, by definition, 'unscientific'. It follows therefore that what orthodox doctors do is based on scientific evidence and what unorthodox practitioners do, whether they be medical or nonmedical, is not.

Is such a definition plausible? Many commonplace examples challenge this idea. For example, is the common practice of prescribing antibiotics for colds and ear infections orthodox or unorthodox, as it is clearly not supported by scientific evidence? In both orthodox and unorthodox medicine it would seem there is no evidence for many commonly used practices and little evidence for others.

What is the relationship between evidence and practice?

Many things taught as 'standard practice' for generations in medical education have only been loosely based on evidence. Take the routine hospital admission of women with twin pregnancies between the 26th to the 34th week of gestation. On the basis of 'circumstantial evidence' it was assumed that such a technological and expensive intervention was justified because it was assumed to reduce complications and premature labour. It often takes a long time for a study on the outcomes of common medical procedures to be done. In fact, when outcomes on this practice were looked at, the evidence showed that all indicators for morbidity, premature labour and perinatal mortality were higher for women who were routinely admitted compared to those who stayed at home and had regular checkups.[1,2]

It is also well known that generations of women were subjected to radical and deforming surgery for breast cancer when there was scant if any evidence that such surgery improved outcomes compared to more conservative surgery. Less well known is the fact that prostate symptoms have very little to do with prostate size according to the 'Australian Guidelines on Lower Urinary Tract Symptoms in Men' put out by the NH&MRC.[3]

Medical practice is often, but far from always, formulated on the best available evidence at the time. It would seem, however, that orthodox medicine is often a little too ready to find new ways of intervening without questioning itself with the same rigour and outcome data that it expects from unorthodox medicine. It is in no way wrong that we wish to see evidence for practices which fall outside of the present medical model but sometimes we need to be a little more self critical.

One must attend in medical practice not
primarily to plausible theories but to experience
combined with reason.

Hippocrates

We often understand little about the mechanisms behind unorthodox approaches as they frequently do not fit within accepted scientific paradigms. The fact that we know little about them, however, does not mean they are not efficacious. As an example there were surprising results of a meta-analysis in the Lancet examining the controlled trials on homeopathy.[4] It showed a very high proportion of studies yielding positive effects greater than placebo. In Europe, where most of the studies have been done and reported, homeopathy is quite widely used by the public and medical profession.[5] We know little about the mechanisms behind homeopathy but that is a limitation upon our present knowledge rather than the natural phenomenon being studied. More constructive than dismissing the evidence out of hand is to search into the laws behind it. Although homeopathy is hard to understand in the usual biomedical way, there are many precedents in the biomedical literature to support the fundamental tenets.[6]

The intention here is not to get involved in a complicated debate as to the efficacy or otherwise of homeopathy but rather to raise questions. Many things are taken for granted now which at the time of their original discovery and investigation were mysterious and challenged the then existing paradigms. How many times have new ways of thinking been rejected out of hand for prolonged periods of time despite evidence? Acupuncture was at one time considered unorthodox but is now coming within the boundary line due to mounting evidence. We still know very little about the mechanisms behind it, although there is evidence that the mysterious acupuncture meridians do actually exist. Meditation is similarly gaining wider acceptance. Orthodox acceptance, however is often slowed by entrenched patterns of thought. Homeopathy, acupuncture and meditation all challenge us to think about the body, energy and mind in more flexible ways.

As doctors we are often hard to convince about things which fall outside our paradigms but are too easily convinced about things which fall inside them. Aspirin has very quickly become accepted as standard care for people with ischaemic heart disease and is promoted by some as prophylaxis for the general population and yet there is much evidence to suggest that benefits are less than one would have hoped for. For many people the benefits are offset by equal levels of harm, for example reduced heart attacks are offset by increased numbers of strokes for those with even mildly raised blood pressure.[7] Another area which reflects this, has been a significant push by many orthodox practitioners for the widespread use of hormone replacement therapy (HRT) for menopausal women. But is it reasonable to treat a natural phase of the lifecycle as if it were a pathological process? While selected women at high risk for osteoporosis or suffering extreme menopausal symptoms, may benefit from HRT in the short term, the long term effects are unknown.

These issues may be a significant reason as to why people are increasingly looking outside the medical model for their healthcare.[8–10] One of the most important reasons for the use of unconventional therapies is concern about side effects and costs of orthodox medical treatments,[11] and the fact that unorthodox practitioners generally spend more time on lifestyle, education and the therapeutic relationship. Unfortunately the structure of the system in which many orthodox practitioners work make it difficult for them to do this.

Often predating fundamental shifts in medical practice and resource allocation are radical shifts in thinking. It is hard to be reflective about our own practice and to absorb new evidence if we do not have both open and critical minds.

Conclusion

Perhaps a more accurate definition of orthodox medicine is 'what is commonly done by doctors' or 'what is accepted to be consistent with our current paradigms or scientific dogma'. It seems that orthodox medicine has far less to do with objectivity or science than we would generally like to think. As doctors and medical educators we will have to take great care to preserve our scientific objectivity and common sense lest history repeats itself. One would not like to condemn or mock modern day Galileos who are guilty of challenging the orthodoxy of the day on the basis of rejecting evidence which could not be accommodated within a limited paradigm. The religion of yesteryear is often seen as being dogmatic and antiprogress but perphaps science, which is the religion of today for many, often demonstrates many of the same traits.

The risks and benefits of complementary medicine

In recent times I have come across two quotations on the potential benefits and dangers of keeping an open mind.

'The mind is like a parachute. In order to work it needs to be open.'

Author unknown

'You need to keep an open mind — but not so open that your brain falls out.'

A MacLennan, Professor of O&G,
University of Adelaide.

If we could not keep our minds open new scientific discoveries and improved methods of practice would be impossible. It takes a new way of thinking or looking to improve on present knowledge and past practice. On the other hand, we often walk a fine line between discovery and gullibility when exploring new areas of knowledge. We should not be too ready to believe or disbelieve what we read.

One area that challenges so called orthodox or traditional medicine is the current trend to 'complementary medicine'. This large and diverse group of modalities* is sometimes called 'natural medicine,' because it relies on an ethos of 'working with nature' and using naturally occurring products, or 'alternative medicine' because these therapies were seen as alternatives to traditional medicine. In more recent times complementary and integrative medicine are the commonly used terms, implying that these modalities are to complement orthodox medical practice or be integrated into it. Mind you, trying to define what constitutes 'orthodox' is just as difficult as trying to determine what is unorthodox, because we find that doctors practise in such diverse ways — ways that are often contrary to established practice guidelines, whether it involves the management of prostate disease, hypertension or breast cancer.[1-3] This is not to say that doctors are necessarily practising unsafely or incompetently, but perhaps it is an indication that the doctor has to balance up many factors which do not appear in guidelines and require varying levels of skill and experience.

Whatever we think of complementary medicine we cannot ignore its presence or deny that the general public are becoming increasingly interested in it. The public may be aware of new scientific research but more often the evidence they regard first and foremost is their own clinical trial of one patient, ie. themselves. 'Does it work for me or not?' In recent Australian data it was found that between 48.5 and 57% of the public were using some form or other of natural medicines.[4,5] The patient's financial outlay for these forms of medicine was also found to rival outlay for pharmaceutical drugs. The patients who chose complementary medicine were more likely to be better educated, wealthier, younger and female. Similar trends are being reported elsewhere in the world.[6] In fact, in Europe there is a generally far higher acceptance of complementary medicine than here. Furthermore, in the US it has recently been demonstrated that 64% of medical courses have content on it.[7] In Australia, at Monash University for example, there are a series of options and forums throughout the course. These tend to be the most popular options.

What are the reasons that the public are turning to complementary medicine? One study concluded that patients were not generally dissatisfied with orthodox medicine.[8] The more pressing reasons were that the 'natural' or 'holistic' approach was more akin to them philosophically and culturally.

> *'Health is caused in a sick man, sometimes by an exterior principle, namely, by the medical art; sometimes by an interior principle, as when a man is healed by the force of nature. ... Just as nature heals a man by alteration, digestion, rejection of the matter that caused the sickness, so does art. ... The exterior principle, art, acts not as a primary agent, but as helping the primary agent, which is the interior principle, and by furnishing it with instruments and assistance, of which the interior principle makes use in producing the effect. Thus the physician strengthens nature, and employs food and medicine, of which nature makes use for the intended end.'*

> Thomas Aquinas
> (1225–1274, Italian philosopher and theologian)

Also very significant in patients' choice of medicine was whether they had a transformational experience which changed their world view. It was also found that certain medical conditions were strongly associated with a search for alternatives; these included anxiety, back problems, chronic pain and urinary conditions.[8]

What of the therapies themselves? Today we are rightly interested in evidence based medicine. Complementary medicine needs to be tested, but study designs need to be sensitive to the peculiarities of the particular modality. Such research is likely to always find it harder to attract funding as it is a lot harder to wind up with a patentable product at the end of the research. Though we have a long way to go, inroads are being made. The National Institute of Health in the USA recently issued a policy statement saying that the evidence base for the use of acupuncture in a number of conditions is sufficiently strong to give it official approval. As another example, a recent meta analysis in the Lancet yielded a surprising result on the efficacy of homeopathy.[9] It found that the odds ratio for a positive result was 2.45 (95% CI 2.05, 2.93) in favour of homeopathy when the suitable 89 placebo-controlled trials were included; (ie. trials were nearly two and a half times more likely to show a positive statistical result than not). Though more research is still needed there is clearly some clinical effect taking place, and we, with our Western models of science, struggle to understand the mechanism of action.**

Are there lessons to learn?

What are some of the salient lessons for us? Four come to mind.

- First, I suspect we need to be sensitive to the philosophical and cultural views of our patients more than in the past.
- Second, we should not be too quick to accept or reject evidence, whether the source is patient experience or clinical trials.
- Third, we need to value the patient–therapist relationship as much as the patient does.
- Last, perhaps we need to shift the debate from an adversarial one, between apparently opposing factions to one that simply focuses on whatever works so that discussion remains objective, constructive and respectful.

To dismiss complementary medicine out of hand rather than try to distil the best and safest elements of it might do us more harm than good as a profession. But if these lessons are learned then the current trend towards complementary medicine may be useful for many reasons. It may provide many GPs with valuable new strings to add to their therapeutic bows and also it may have led us to be much more reflective and questioning about modern medicine, however it is defined.[10–12]

GPs interested in finding out more about complementary medicine and integrative medicine should contact the

Australian Integrative Medicine Association or the Swinburne University Graduate School of Integrative Medicine, both through Swinburne University in Victoria, or the Research Unit for Complementary Medicine at the University of Western Sydney, Macarthur, in NSW.

Contemplative practices and healing

The practical aspects

What is meditation?

There are many ways of expressing what comprises a meditative exercise, depending on which aspect of the process is emphasised. There is a common misconception that relaxation and meditation exercises are about going to sleep. A truly contemplative or meditative exercise is about 'waking up' or 'tuning the mind in' although it may assist the induction and quality of sleep. However, if one is practising for relaxation of mental and physical tension then it might be called a relaxation exercise.

In cultivating objectivity and detached observation it can also be seen as an exercise in enhancing autonomy, self-control or effective action. The respected researcher, John Kabat-Zinn, describes meditation as a *'way of being'* by helping a person go more deeply into themselves beyond all the surface physical sensations and mental activity. Similarly, some call the meditative process a practice in centring as suggested by T S Elliot's phrase, 'The still point of the turning world.' There, as in the unmoving centre of a wheel, we learn to be still and watch movements in mind and body. Meditation can also be seen as a spiritual exercise or an exercise in self knowledge. In light of this Shakespeare's speech in Hamlet takes on a greater sense of meaning as he asks the 'big question' and describes the state of mind which clouds his judgment and wellbeing.

> *To be or not to be, that is the question. ...*
> *Thus the native hue of resolution*
> *Is sicklied o'er with the pale cast of thought.*

Dealing with the mind

We are often unaware of the nature and extent of mental activity in our minds. It makes itself obvious when we try to concentrate. How often have we noticed that while reading a book our minds are far away, or while driving we are not paying attention, or while conversing with someone we are listening to the conversation in our heads rather than what the person is actually saying? Much of this incessant 'thinking', albeit unconscious, is behind our anxieties and fears and makes us inefficient and less effective. To be free of it we must first be aware of it, consciously examine it and then be detached from it. It will not loosen its influence unless we let it go. For this reason cognitive behaviour therapies (CBT) can be greatly enhanced by such exercises as they help us sift out what is unnecessary, untrue or unhelpful.

Most meditative techniques rely on the attention being focused restfully on a focal point; hence the term 'restful alertness.' In order to do this one need not struggle with a distracting stream of circular, habitual, repetitive and imaginary mental activity. One quickly learns that we cannot 'stop the mind from thinking' and any attempt to do so generally leads to tension and frustration. We can, however, learn not to be so reactive to it. This takes the emotive force out of it and, in due course, allows us to 'transcend' it. Analogously, the depressed, distracted or anxious mind is populated with thoughts which behave like barking dogs. If one tries to run from them they pursue us and if one fights with them they bite. If one doesn't react then they go away in their own time leaving us in peace.

The creative process

As a man (or woman) thinketh,
so he (or she) becomes.

JAMES ALLEN

The primary source of creative potential, before anything mental or physical manifests itself, is described as consciousness, attention or awareness. A more materialist view may well see it the other way around. Metaphorically, consciousness is often referred to as 'light' because of its ability to make things seen and this concept is reflected in a great deal of our common language. At a very low level of awareness we feel like we are 'in the dark', for example when we suddenly understand something we previously couldn't, we say that it is 'very illuminating.'

What we give our attention to is important as it gives thoughts and emotions the power to manifest themselves. For example, by giving much attention to fearful, anxious, angry or depressing thoughts we almost 'meditate' upon them progressively, making them more 'real' and compelling. Over time they can clearly be demonstrated to change the brain's chemistry setting up a cascade of events throughout the body. This is one of the problems with the mind's tendency to visualise, ruminate and imagine. When we take such imaginings and mental projections to be real they govern our lives, behaviour and responses to events.

We do not see things as they are.
We see them as we are.

Talmud

Such unhelpful, repetitive, habitual, often compelling and unconscious mental activity is at the source of much of our stress and maladaptive coping strategies. We easily lose the ability to distinguish between reality and imagination and start running from imaginary stressors. If we reduce the effect of such self-inflicted stressors we have more energy and awareness to give to the ones which are really there. Some of the 'side effects' of meditation include:

- learning to determine the difference between reality and mental projection,
- to gently 'unhook' the attention from mental ruts and compulsions, and
- to live more consciously by focusing on our lives from moment to moment. The practical benefits will flow in due course but it takes practice and patience. It is not necessarily a 'quick fix'.

The relaxation response

Eliciting a more relaxed state of being can be done in a number of ways. Creativity, hobbies, regular physical exercise and some forms of music are commonly used methods. Gaining wider popularity are techniques like Tai Chi and Yoga which combine mental focus with physical movement. Also used are techniques such as hypnosis and biofeedback. In religious settings significant benefits are associated with prayer or confession, whereas in the secular setting open communication, psychotherapy and counselling can produce benefits.

Meditation is certainly a well studied and, when practised with care, is a very potent way of eliciting the 'relaxation response'. There are a variety of meditation practices (*see next page*). Obviously we cannot 'meditate our problems away' so it must be used in conjunction with a rational and conscious approach to problem solving in daily life. Different forms of meditation suit different people but they all need practice and perseverance in order to be effective. Like physical exercise the benefits are cumulative and it should not be expected always to be easy. That it is sometimes difficult does not mean that it is not useful.

The relaxation response does not perform magic; it simply helps to undo the harmful effects of inappropriate stress, thereby letting the physiology return to a healthy balance. It

Meditation practices

Some commonly used varieties of meditation and relaxation exercises:

1. Mindfulness. See below.

2. Progressive muscle relaxation. Physical muscle tension is methodically released.

3. Mantra meditation. The mantra, as the focus of restful concentration, is a word or short phrase repeated silently in the mind which progressively takes the mind beyond the usual mental agitation. It has been practised in most cultures, such as in the East or ancient Christian traditions, often, but not always, as a spiritual discipline. It has also been adapted to a secular environment.

4. Visualisation, affirmations and imagery. These can help to refocus a distracted or anxious mind to some extent, reinforce attitude change and tap into unconscious thought patterns and memories.

should be noted that meditation is more than just physical relaxation for it engages mind as well as body. Pure physical relaxation, as beneficial as it is, is like a doorway to meditative practices.

Mindfulness meditation

This technique is easy to adapt in the health setting for both groups and individuals. As a stress reduction technique it has been well shown to be powerfully therapeutic. Controlled trials where groups, including medical students, were given a mindfulness stress management program[1,2] showed advantages of reduced anxiety, distress and depression, and increased empathy, self control and spiritual experiences. It is important that meditation is made practical, simple and relevant to the individual's needs and not introduced in a way which is culturally threatening. The aspect which is relevant to the person is the one that is emphasised, not the agenda of the person teaching it. It can be used by itself or as an adjunct to counselling or cognitive and behavioural therapies. Contraindications are few but include major psychological disturbances such as

Ways of punctuating the day with mindfulness meditation

Full stops
- Initially practise for five minutes twice daily (before eating is preferable).
- Build up to 10–30 minutes twice daily if motivated.

Preparation
- One can practice anywhere, any time, but it may be more of a challenge in a noisy environment so a quiet place free from disturbance is optimal.

Position
- An upright, relaxed and balanced spine is the most conducive posture. Lying down can be comfortable but the ease of going to sleep may not always be desirable.
- Let the eyes close.

Progressive muscle relaxation
- Becoming aware of one particular part of the body at a time, starting with the feet. Gently let go of any muscle tension there.
- Then move the awareness to the legs and relax. So on to the stomach, back, hands, arms, shoulders, neck and face.
- If you become aware of tension coming back simply let it go again.
- Try not to force it but just 'let' the relaxation happen.

Breathing
- Now simply feel the breath as it passes in and out of the body.
- There is no need to regulate or control the breath.
- If distracting thoughts and feelings come into the mind, carrying the attention away with them, just be aware of them but let them go.
- There is no need to try and stop these thoughts coming into mind, nor to try forcing them out. This only feeds them with attention and makes them stronger. Just be less reactive to them.
- After a time move to the listening.

Listening
- Practise the same restful attentiveness with the sense of hearing.
- Be aware of the sounds in the environment both near and far.
- Once again let any thoughts or feelings come and go.

Finishing
- After practising for the allotted time gently move back into the activities which await you.

Commas
- These involve the same steps as above but only for a shorter time.
- Regular short practices of just a few seconds (with a few deep and relaxing breaths) to a few minutes during the day can greatly reinforce relaxation and mindfulness. It is ideal for busy lives.

psychosis and major personality disorder. Furthermore, even though meditation helps with depression and anxiety it may still need to be used in conjunction with pharmaceutical treatment especially for severe cases.

A day without some time for conscious rest is like an unpunctuated book; it becomes a blur and makes little sense. A couple of very effective ways of 'punctuating' one's day are listed (*see previous page*).

Conclusion

In closing, we could return to the question as to why people have always developed and practised various contemplative exercises. Perhaps the short answer to the question is that people use them because they work. Scientific investigation of them is both necessary and useful and philosophical reflection about them is interesting and insightful but ultimately the only proof which carries any weight is our direct personal experience.

To be or not to be

Evidence in support of contemplative practices

Why have people throughout recorded history and across various cultures developed and utilised such a variety of contemplative and meditative practices? When people wish to increase productivity, efficiency or performance, why do they practise relaxation? How can something so simple as meditation have such a potent healing potential?

What is a contemplative practice?

The etymology of contemplation is interesting. In Latin it is made up of two words. The first comes from the prefix 'con–' and literally means 'to join with'. The second word is '–templum' from which the word temple is derived and literally means 'a large space for observation'. Temples also carry connotations of openness, quietude and sanctity. So the activity of contemplation involves uniting with some expansive faculty of observation, in other words the conscious aspect of our being.

In modern usage, contemplation and meditation take on a sense of quiet consideration of some issue, concentration, reflection or absorption. Such a mental state is often associated with a deep sense of quiet happiness, intuition, self knowledge, connectedness and inner peace. Correspondingly on the physical level there is an increase of efficiency and harmony in the body's physiology.

Meditation's power to heal

Recently I was once again struck with meditation's ability to restore balance and reverse disease processes. In a landmark study[1] patients with cerebrovascular disease (CVD) were divided into intervention and control groups with the intervention group taking up transcendental meditation for 20 minutes twice a day. The control group had a CVD health education program aimed at lowering risk factors and also were encouraged to spend 20 minutes a day in relaxing leisure activities other than meditation. What was found over the 6–9 month follow up was that the meditation group were reversing their vascular disease (0.1 mm average reduction in intima thickening of the carotid arteries) compared to the control group whose disease advanced (by an average of 0.05 mm). The improvements were not attributable to changes in other cardiovascular risk factors. Such reductions in arterial wall thickness would translate into reductions of risk of acute myocardial infarction of 11% and of stroke of 15%. Larger and more prolonged studies are needed to fully measure the cumulative effects of meditation on CVD.

The effects of prolonged and excessive psychological stress on the body involves every system, so it would seem reasonable to expect that the benefits of effectively reversing stress will also involve every system of the body. The fact that stress can increase blood pressure is widely known but it is less well known that chronic stress can slow wound healing,[2] increase genetic mutations[3] and slow repair.[4] Stress also effects genetic expression which can predispose to problems as diverse as addictive behaviours,[5] cardiovascular reactivity,[6] depression[7] and schizophrenia.[8]

The first proof of a well ordered mind is to be able
to pause and linger within itself.

Seneca

Physiological benefits of relaxation and stress reduction

- Marked decrease in oxygen consumption, metabolic rate, respiration rate and minute ventilation[12]
- A lowering of catechols and receptor sensitivity[13,14]
- Reduction in blood pressure and heart rate[15]
- Reduction in serum cholesterol, increase in skin resistance (low skin resistance is an accurate marker of stress responses), decrease in blood lactate[16]
- Changes in EEG patterns including an increase in alpha and theta waves and EEG coherence (coordination of EEG waves)[17]
- A reduction in epileptic seizure frequency[18]
- A suggested selective increase in cerebral blood flow[19]
- Reduction in cortisol levels which may help to reverse the increased calcium loss and osteoporosis associated with high cortisol levels[20]
- Reduced TSH and T3 levels[21] (Thyroid hormones)
- Increased melatonin which has oncostatic effects, enhances immune function and reduces jetlag[22,23]
- Improved immune function through reversal of the immunosuppressive effects of stress[24,25]
- An adjunct to therapy for a variety of illnesses such as cardiovascular disease, cancer, chronic pain,[26] asthma,[27] diabetes.[28]

It seems that this calmer and more orderly mental state is mirrored physically. Some of the other reversible physical and psychological effects of stress and benefits of meditation are presented in *Physiological benefits of relaxation and stress reduction (above)* and *Psychological benefits of stress reduction (opposite page)*.

Good sense and good economy

Insurance company auditors are happy to leave clinicians and physiologists to work out the mechanisms to explain such observations. They are more interested in the 'bottom line.' Health savings have been mentioned in a previous article[9] but to briefly reiterate: their findings suggest that over an 11 year period they found an overall 63% reduction in healthcare costs. This was made up of 11.4 times fewer hospital admissions for CVD, 3.3 times fewer for cancer and 6.7 times fewer for mental disorders and substance abuse.[10] In these particular studies self selection and healthy lifestyle change would play a part in the results and so the benefits are probably explained by these factors along with the direct physiological benefits. Healthy lifestyle change is not unrelated to a more peaceful, conscious and autonomous mental state. Feeling more autonomous (ie. having greater self control) seems to be a vital prerequisite to making and maintaining healthy lifestyle change. Contemporary evidence suggests that lifestyle advice without fostering the ability to implement it provides little long term health benefit.[11] Historically, however, the relationship between mindfulness or awareness and autonomy has long been recognised.

Eternal vigilance is the price of liberty

John Curran

Psychological benefits of stress reduction

- Decreased anxiety[29,30]
- Better pain control[26]
- More optimism, less depression as indicated by elevation of serotonin[31,32]
- Greater self awareness and self actualisation[33]
- Improved coping capabilities[34]
- Improved wellbeing and as an adjunct to psychotherapy[35]
- Reduced reliance upon drugs, prescribed and nonprescribed, or alcohol[36]
- Improved sleep[37]
- Reduced aggression and criminal tendency[38]
- Greater efficiency and output and reduced stress at work[39]
- Improved response time and reflexes[40]
- Improvement in perceptiveness of hearing and other senses[41]
- Improved concentration and memory[42,43]
- Facilitation of healthy change of undesired personality traits[44]

On the strength of the evidence, insurance companies in the USA and Europe are starting to offer substantial reductions on life insurance premiums of up to 30% for people who practise an approved form of meditation regularly, in this case transcendental meditation.

Conclusion

A drug with proven efficacy and a good side effect profile would be widely promoted. The slowness to take up such research may be multifactorial. Perhaps the mechanisms for the changes are yet to be fully elucidated. It may be that simple solutions are an affront to our faith in technological solutions to human problems. There is also a degree of stigma and misinformation surrounding the practice of meditation. This will probably change with ongoing evidence, responsible use and well grounded education, but it will take time.

The economy of health

Most doctors are very conscious of escalating health care costs and the need to limit expenditure. At every step one gets the sense, whether real or perceived, that resources are scarce. The problem touches everybody. There are significant cost increases in medical indemnity, escalating health insurance, restrictions on prescribing and ordering of pathology and radiology tests and limited access to medical resources and community supports. It often appears like a financial, administrative and clinical nightmare. Balanced against this must be an acknowledgment of the difficult position of health economists and governments. There are many competing needs in the community and resources are limited.

One must also acknowledge the great advances of medical technology.[1] One down side is that it has resulted in modern medicine consuming resources at an alarming rate. There are also examples of the medical industry harming itself with a mentality more driven by profit than need, compassion or patient care.

Various methods have been designed to rationally answer resource allocation questions — such as the complex Quality Adjusted Life Year (QALY) measure. It attempts to put figures on incalculable things like existence, happiness, and suffering.

Like comparing oranges with apples it also tries to compare different forms of treatment such as cardiac bypass surgery and hip replacement.

The right answers need the right questions

But are we even asking the right questions? Does the system really need more money or is it more a problem of how the money is distributed? Does our fascination for technology sometimes lead us to ignore options that are less dramatic but have better long term outcomes? Are we treating the illnesses we should be preventing?

As an illustration, the health budget of Victoria for 1997–1998 allocated $2400 million for acute health services (nearly 50% of the state's health budget)[2] whereas only $50–100 million (1–2%) was spent on health promotion. Estimates vary depending on how you define health promotion activities. For comparison there was nearly $192 million spent on the number one selling drug in Australia, simvastatin, in 1998.[3] Nearly all the top ten selling drugs are for conditions that are significantly amenable to lifestyle treatment.

The benefits of lifestyle change

The role of nature and lifestyle in healing is possibly much undervalued in modern health care. This was not so in the past. Many centuries ago Thomas Aquinas discussed the relationship between the medical art of the doctor (secondary or exterior principle) and the body's natural ability for self healing (primary or interior principle).

> *The exterior principle, art, acts not as a primary agent, but as helping the primary agent, which is the interior principle, and by furnishing it with instruments and assistance, of which the interior principle makes use in producing the effect. Thus the physician strengthens nature, and employs food and medicine, of which nature makes use for the intended end.*
>
> Thomas Aquinas

In the contemporary context it is interesting to examine applications of this simple philosophy. It is well known that lifestyle interventions are powerful therapeutic tools. This can be done in a variety of ways including individual and population based interventions. For example, one study showed that 'one on one' dietary counselling from a doctor and dietician led to an average sustained weight loss of 6.7 kg per patient (at a cost of $9.76 per kg)! There were also significant reductions in blood pressure compared with controls.[4] A population study examining a community based coronary heart disease health promotion project over a 4 year period was associated with an almost 7% quit rate for smoking and healthy dietary changes when compared with controls. The cost per life year gained was £31.[5] Evidence further shows that interventions for reducing cardiovascular risk are also effective when implemented in workplaces.[6]

Other interventions target different age groups. For example much evidence suggests that exercise in the elderly can prevent osteoporosis[7,8] and hip fracture.[9] Not only are the side effects of exercise good but, again, it also reduces costs. Educational interventions directed at doctors about the benefits of exercise for the elderly are associated with significant benefits in their patient populations.[10] Interventions for school children demonstrate that they are effective although long term follow up is required.[11]

Helping the mind is also important. For example, a stress management intervention for frequent attenders to family physicians showed a 50% reduction in attendances and an average cost saving of US$3900 per patient over the 6 months of the study compared with controls.[12] Elsewhere it has been found through examining 11 years of insurance company archival data covering 600 000 people that an Ayurvedic† approach to lifestyle was associated with an overall 63% reduction of health care utilisation. This included 11.4 times less CHD, 3.3 times less cancer and 6.7 times less mental illness and substance abuse in the intervention group.[13] Needless to say insurance companies are

---

Keypoints

- To take a long term view to health care quality and cost cutting we may need to allocate more resources to health promotion and holistic interventions.
- The appropriate use of many technologies can reduce health care costs. Indiscriminate use can cause needless expense and patient burden.
- Many current strategies and practices driven by short term views are expensive in the long run.
- Most of the impetus for change is coming from the general community and the health insurance industry who are, by and large, driven by different motivation from the health care industry. Clinicians and patients often get caught in the crossfire.
- Technology and pharmaceuticals have an important place but that should, wherever possible, be secondary to the inexpensive primary foundations of good health (ie. lifestyle and psychosocial factors).
- If policy makers sincerely wish to promote health in the community then the system must be conducive to this: (eg. altering billing systems, rewarding longer consultations and possibly encouraging small group education by family physicians as well as targeting individuals and populations).

---

becoming very interested in such approaches and in some countries they are offering substantial reductions on life insurance premiums for people who use them.

Even when treating advanced disease there is still clear evidence that simple lifestyle measures and holistic approaches combined with the usual care are far more effective than usual care alone in terms of outcomes, quality of life and reduced costs. The Ornish Program for CHD, which included a low fat vegetarian diet, stress management, group support, meditation, stopping smoking and moderate exercise was shown angiographically and symptomatically to reverse CHD. It also reduced ongoing cardiac events by a factor of 2.5 over a 5 year follow up.[14,15] The control group showed worsening CHD with more requiring bypass surgery or dying. The savings associated with the Ornish approach were estimated in 1993 to be $58 000 per cardiac patient.[16] Once again the insurance companies and general public were more interested in promoting these programs than the medical community.

It would seem that ignoring simple, common sense and natural principles is an expensive exercise in every way. Unless we learn the lessons soon the health care system may be crushed under the weight of its own expense. Neither doctors nor patients would like to see that!

† Ayurveda is a Sanskrit word meaning 'life knowledge'. Its ancient origins are from India and entails a holistic lifestyle including transcendental meditation.

Evidence – whose evidence?

The corporatisation of medical research

It is strange how things often happen in threes. So it was with a recent series of events. The first was a discussion with a colleague who had recently been funded to undertake research into the efficacy of a device which was popularly advertised as effective for a particular condition. The research was duly done with great care with regards to the methodology and data analysis. The result? The device had no clinical effect. The upshot? The company which markets and promotes the device is attempting at each turn to prevent publication of the results. This raises the following questions :
- Whose evidence is it?
  - Is it the company's who funded it?
  - Is it the researcher's who researched it?
  - Is it the community's whose money and health are on the line?
- Is there a duty to publish negative findings?

The second episode occurred a few days later with an invitation to look over a research proposal. The research was to compare the efficacy of a drug against its efficacy plus a psychosocial intervention. It was suggested that it would be useful to have a third arm of the study evaluating the psychosocial intervention alone. The response was that the idea, although useful in terms of the research, was not a prospect that the drug company would consider funding. The reason? They would not like to find a nondrug treatment as good as. or better than. the drug treatment.

The third episode involved the June 5 (2000) edition of the ABC's Health Report. This was an examination of how the news media present stories on the benefits and risks of medications.[1] Journalist Ray Moynihan reported the results of his recently published paper in the prestigious *New England Journal of Medicine.*[2] Interestingly,this journal had some time before come under criticism for not disclosing the financial ties of its medical writers. This research resulted from a concern at how easily the 'PR machines' of the drug companies could put a spin on the results of research findings, and that press releases are often presented like 'news stories'. Moynihan's team 'studied the coverage in the U.S. news media of the risks and benefits of three medications which are used to prevent major diseases.' This involved 207 news stories over 1994–8. Perhaps their findings were not surprising but, when you consider their implications, they are a little disconcerting. (*see below*)

The author's conclusions were: News media stories about medications may include inadequate or incomplete information about the benefits, risks, and costs of the drugs as well as the

---

Main findings of the Moynihan et al study into US news coverage of the risks and benefits of medications

- Forty percent of stories did not report benefits quantitatively.
- Of those that did, 83% reported relative benefits only; 2% reported absolute benefits only; and 15% reported absolute and relative benefits.
- Only 47% mentioned potential harm to patients.
- Only 30% mentioned costs.
- Of those that cited an expert or a scientific study, 50% cited an expert or study with a financial tie to the manufacturer of the drug.
- These ties were only cited in 39% of the stories

---

financial ties between study groups or experts and pharmaceutical manufacturers.

Selective presentation of the facts

It is not just what you say but how you say it, and to an unsuspecting or untrained listener, reader or viewer, results often seem a lot more impressive than they really are. An interesting example involved a promotion for the drug Fosamax, which is used to prevent osteoporosis and hip fracture. This promotion claimed that Fosamax could reduce the incidence of osteoporosis by 50%. It sounds impressive. But this is the relative benefit only. The absolute benefit is that it reduced the risk from 2% to 1% which, although it is a 50% reduction, sounds far less impressive, especially when one considers the frequently unmentioned costs, alternatives and side effects.

Elsewhere it has been shown that researchers with drug company funding are much more likely to report positive findings from their research than those without drug company funding.[3] The reasons could be many including:

• biased research
• companies funding researchers who are getting positive results and withholding publication of negative findings.

From the above example, it appears that 'evidence' is not always what it seems to be and 'evidence based medicine', while being innately a worthwhile aim, has a human confounder which needs to be accounted for if one wants to pursue truth in medical science. In the meantime doctors and patients must be cautious in how they interpret the 'information' which comes their way.

Paying the piper

What is also of concern is that as funding for universities is gradually cut back, there is a risk they will need to court the corporate dollar. As corporatisation weighs heavily on the scales there is the risk that scientific objectivity will weigh relatively less. What are the implications for research and clinical medicine? Are only those things which can be patented and marketed likely to attract funds and publicity? Will research which potentially reduces health care costs or reliance on pharmaceuticals be able to attract funds? Conflicts of interest are easy to envisage.

The next wave on the horizon, and it is a very big one in terms of potential conflict between financial and scientific imperatives, is that of genetic engineering. Already there is a significant concern in the community that science is being driven by multinational company profit more than by concern for the interests of the community. Are the potential benefits being overplayed? What hope is there of companies funding or publishing research into the potentially harmful effects of such technologies? How will we find out anyway? Will it take a major and unpredictable 'catastrophe' to turn the tide?

How to maintain safeguards

At the very time that one would hope scientific and academic institutions are increasing scrutiny and safeguards it would appear that some are softening them. This is illustrated by Harvard University, which modified it's guidelines so as to allow greater financial ties between researchers and the companies which make the products they are researching.[4] The concern for the university is that the lucrative contracts will lure the best people away from organisations which have the strictest guidelines.

It would seem that by a slow and steady commercialisation of the health care profession (industry) there is an ever growing risk that the primary focus will shift from patient and community care to profit making from benefit to the patient and community, to benefit to the large corporations. Corporatisation works on every scale of medical care. Although not popular with many GPs, general practices are continually being swallowed up by corporations according to an Australian Federal

Government review. Large tertiary hospitals are becoming 'Health care networks' which many people see as uncaring or impersonal. The loosening of laws around advertising has already opened the gate to claims of false advertising. On it goes.

When essential services privatise there is often a sense that profit rather than service is the key issue, with service being sacrificed. But in relation to information provision the issue can become potentially very deceptive. 'Infomercials' are often hard to tell from real news and 'cash for comments' have damaged radio station and presenter integrity. Laws are now being passed in many countries to ensure that advertising is transparent.

Conclusion

There may be more at stake than we realise. Conflicts of interest when the public's health and wellbeing are at stake do not go down well with the community, and for good reason. How such dilemmas can be addressed may be a complex issue, especially if we do not get the first principles right. One would not wish to argue against a sensible relationship between the corporate and health care worlds but for this relationship to work one suspects that it must recognise the fact that their respective languages, aims, motivations and ethics are unique to each. To make it work may involve complicated legislation and safeguards or perhaps just needs a shift in community values or will. After all, this is what laws, customs and practices will follow.

Psychoneuroimmunology

A Platonic view of the immune system

The classic text, Plato's *Republic*, is a lengthy discourse on the nature of justice. The Greeks encompassed a very broad definition of justice with notions like good, harmony, balance and health. The *Republic* includes a description of the nature and education of the 'guardians of the state' who administered the state for the good of all. They recognised friend from foe, were courageous, temperate, reasonable and peace loving, and were duty bound to selflessly lay down their lives for that purpose. If the guardians did their job well then the state lived in health, happiness and harmony with the citizens able to get on with the business of daily living protected from malignant influences.

For the greater good

Plato's description of the nature and behaviour of the guardians of the state uncannily parallels the nature and behaviour of the guardians of the body, the immune system, made up of cells whose function is to give their lives for the protection and integrity of the body. The field of science which we now call psychoneuroimmunology (PNI) is detailing what we have known for a long time, namely that the state of mind affects the state of the immune system. A healthy mind closely corresponds with a healthy body although our elucidation of the biochemical pathways is catching up to our understanding of the principle.

The mechanisms which connect mind and immune system, such as through the hypopituitary axis, are rich and varied. Direct communication between the CNS and the immune cells is taking place all the time, effecting the function of each. It takes place directly via the synapsing of neurones with white blood cells (WBCs) in lymphoid tissues and indirectly through blood-borne neurotransmitters and hormones stimulating receptors on the surface of WBCs. WBCs also feed back to the brain, especially to the limbic system associated with emotion. As we would expect, fear, stress, anger and depression are not associated with good immune function, whereas happiness, calm and clarity are.

'The arrival of a good clown exercises more beneficial influence upon the health of a town than that of twenty asses laden with drugs.'

Dr Thomas Sydenham

'A merry heart doeth good like a medicine but a broken spirit drieth the bones.'

Proverbs

'There is no reason for any panic. Fear is cowardly and very injurious. Cheerfulness increases resistance and prevents complications.'

Public Health Bulletin: 1919 Influenza Epidemic

Such mechanisms are very fully described in some excellent books on the subject.[1,2] Despite such huge promise the clinical implications of PNI are little known by the wider medical community.

Response of the immune system

The crucial criteria the immune system applies, as did Plato's guardians, is to make the distinction between friend and foe, self and not self, benevolent and malignant. Its malfunctions seem to be of three types:

- inappropriate reaction, as in stimulating an immune response to tissues which should not be attacked through a case of mistaken identity, ie. attacking self as if it were not self, eg. auto-immune diseases like inflammatory bowel disease, juvenile onset diabetes or rheumatoid arthritis.
- over-reaction occurs with aggravation of inflammatory or allergic processes such as in asthma or dermatitis.
- under-reaction as in immune suppression, allows germs and cancer cells to slip past the body's many protective surveillance mechanisms.

When life-style and environmental factors combine with genetic disposition we start to appreciate how it is that stress is such an important potential trigger for disease processes to start playing out.

Can mental processes change physical health

The clinical implications of PNI are far reaching. For example it has been observed that when innoculated with the cold virus stressed people are much more likely to catch the cold than less stressed people.[3] Those who are stressed find that they get far poorer immune response to common vaccines such as the flu and Hep B vaccines.[4,5] Elsewhere it has been shown that people could improve immune function through improving their ability to relax or through better emotional expression even if that expression was only keeping a journal about stressful events.[6] The therapeutic potential of this finding has more recently been tested in the observation that patients with a chronic inflammatory condition such as asthma or rheumatoid arthritis can considerably improve their condition by writing in a journal about stressful events.[7] The mechanism seems to have something to do with the stress reduction associated with coming to terms with and understanding traumatic past events. A healthy lifestyle, such as engaging in exercise, managing stress, good quality sleep and diet has been clearly associated with better natural killer cell (NK) function.[8] The role of immune function in cancer is becoming widely recognised. For example we know that the immune system attacks some cancers quite aggressively, like malignant melanoma. It was found that if a 6 week stress management intervention was added to the treatment for early stage melanoma it had the effect of enhancing immune function when compared to controls. After 6 year follow up this translated to a halving of the recurrence rate and more than halving the death rate.[9]

Going back in order to look forward

Happiness, peace and freedom have always been equated a harmonious state of the soul by the ancient Greeks. In fact justice, as described by Plato, was a harmony of the three main elements of the soul:

• reason,
• emotion and
• appetite.

Reason tempers the passionate or emotive element of ourselves which is more than a little apt to 'inflammation' at times when we are ruled by it. This does not underestimate the importance of that emotion or suggest it should be suppressed but rather that reason gives guidance to which emotions should be acted upon and which not. It is interesting to note that similar concepts to Plato's exist in the East. For example, the ancient Eastern language, Sanskrit, has a word for anger, attachment and passion — 'raga'.[10] It also means red and inflammation. The one word tells us many things about psychological states and physical sequelae. Reason also moderates the appetites keeping them in sync with bodily needs. If such a balanced state of the soul exists then health, moderation, efficiency and happiness rule. If one is overruled by the more emotive element then somewhat inflammatory, destructive and unreasonable behaviour ensues. Likewise, if the appetitive element rules, and one overindulges in the pleasures of life, illnesses, in the state or individual, soon abound. Reason is there to deal with or filter unhelpful and harmful ideas and motives. If the guardian, through inattention, does not do its job, then the mind and body are in a somewhat unprotected and vulnerable state. Many of the internal tensions we experience, Plato would have described as a sort of 'civil war' of the soul.

Conclusion

It would seem that 'the body is the shadow of the soul.'[11] Many cognitive and behavioural therapies, of course, seek to strengthen a person's ability to sift through their thoughts and feelings such that they can discard the harmful ones and act on the useful ones. Meditation and other contemplative exercises can facilitate this process enormously. Cultivating a sense of community, civic responsibility and connectedness was also important for Plato so that the whole community and the individual might flourish. Indeed, we are finding that connectedness is enormously protective for physical and emotional health, especially for adolescents.[12] In such a well guarded condition the body or the state could protect its life and in the process live as happily and healthily as possible.

The persona and health

*I would rather know the person who has the
disease than the disease the person has*

Hippocrates

Simple aphorisms like this were the guiding principles for ancient physicians. Sometimes, we become so enamoured with another new drug, surgical procedure or technological advance we neglect the foundations upon which our tradition of medicine is laid.

Hippocrates, like the founders of other ancient healing systems, was essentially holistic. The healer healed body and mind together. He was interested in the patient's emotions, thoughts, fears and personality. To forget the psyche would be like continuously repairing a car without addressing the temperament of the driver.

There is a very large and growing body of scientific evidence to suggest that personality factors have a profound influence upon health status independent of other commonly acknowledged lifestyle risk factors[1] although personality and lifestyle are often related.

It is difficult to be precise about personality typing. No person can be completely pigeonholed and exceptions are always found to every rule, but some general principles do seem to be emerging. Eysenck, who has probably done more work in this field than any other researcher classified personalities as Type 1, 2, 3 and 4. Type 1 are cancer prone with a strong tendency to suppress emotions, feel helpless and hopeless and to deal poorly with interpersonal stress. Type 2 are heart disease prone, tend to be angry and aggressive and also deal poorly with interpersonal stress. Type 4 are not prone to heart disease or cancer and are more 'autonomous'.[2] They are more self-aware, optimistic, relaxed, communicate in a more appropriate way and deal better with interpersonal stress. Type 3 are a mixture of these traits. Eysenck's data are consistent with other findings that personality factors are a good predictor of developing illnesses and have a powerful influence over the progression of an illness. Across all the data, anger seems to be the most 'toxic' emotion whether suppressed or expressed.[3–5]

What is the relevance of this sort of information to doctors and patients? It is easy when suggesting to patients that their coping and communication strategies are putting them at risk of serious illness for them to feel fearful, fatalistic and disempowered. Therefore, it is important to deliver the other side of the story which is quite optimistic and empowering. It is interesting to note that Eysenck took large groups of people who according to their personality traits were heart disease and cancer prone and demonstrated that both the traits and the predisposition to illness could be modified for the better. If you help people to be more self-aware, to objectively and rationally assess behaviour, to practice new strategies for dealing with stress, to communicate better and to relax, you significantly reduce their tendency to get those illnesses when compared to control groups.[2]

The important message is, that our personalities are much more malleable than we think. Our responses tend to become conditioned and so they can be unconditioned. Though we may have largely become creatures of habit we can use 'good habit' to remove 'bad habit'. The remedy for habit is first awareness, then a little detachment (ie. the ability to stand back from the behaviour and watch it), acceptance and then, with that window of choice starting to open, to practise new strategies that help us to feel more in control. Feeling more at peace with our behaviour is almost invariably associated with a more reasonable, clear and emotionally steady way of relating to others.

One of the greatest impediments to constructive personality change is the fear generated from self-criticism, either real or perceived. It keeps us isolated, uncommunicative and continually putting up fronts that we fear will be torn down, to reveal the hurts that lie beneath. In this respect support groups can offer real healing, because it is often when a group starts to open up in a non-judgmental way that we find we have far more in common than we thought. We wrestle with the same issues in a different form and we can learn from the experiences of others and be encouraged by their efforts.

However, even with individuals the doctor can be a powerful instrument for change using an attentive ear, encouragement, a few simple skills and suggestions at the right time. Often just talking about the potential for change is enough to sew the seeds for constructive self-growth that may bear fruit many years hence.

Stress and cancer

*Man is not disturbed by events but by the view
he takes of them.*

Epictetus

If this is true then the reverse may well be true, that is: 'man is not pleased by events but by the view he takes of them'. If one puts these two statements together we might come to the same conclusion as Shakespeare:

*There is nothing either good or bad
but thinking makes it so.*

This article will explore the role of perception in stress and its implications for cancer. These thoughts were produced by two articles which looked at psychosocial factors and their relationship to the causation and progression of cancer. One looked at stressful life events and their correlation with the onset of breast cancer[1] and did not find a connection between the two. The other article demonstrated a significant relationship between psychological response and breast cancer survival[2] in finding that women who measured high on depression scales were 3.59 times as likely to die from all causes over a 5 year follow up (95% CI 1.39–9.24). Those who had high scores for helplessness and hopelessness had a 1.55 times increased recurrence rate (1.07–2.25).

Is the research inconsistent?

The first study's findings are at variance with another large study published in the British Medical Journal in 1995 which found a strong relationship between adverse life events and breast cancer.[3] Kune et al also found a similar relationship for bowel cancer.[4] In Chen's study the increased odds ratio was 3.2 (95% CI 1.35–7.6) and when other factors were controlled the odds ratio rose to 11.6. There is also a strong correlation with other diseases. A study examining the progression of HIV found that for every one severe stressor per 6 month study interval the risk of early disease progression was doubled.[5]

With the public so interested in the role of the mind in the progress of disease, how are we to explain such apparently wide discrepancies and inconsistencies that plague the investigation of psycho-oncology and its sister science of psychoneuroimmunology (PNI)? How are patients, let alone doctors, to make sense of conflicting reports and advice? There may be an important, but sometimes overlooked, piece of the jigsaw puzzle. Apparently conflicting conclusions may not be due to inherent inconsistencies in nature but rather in our inconsistent approach to examining the problem.

Though Protheroe et al discussed life events, it was not clear how the severity of these events were rated, nor was there any evident examination of these women's personalities or coping styles. Were the events rated according to the patient's own perception rather than a rating scale which ignores individual factors? This is important because an event will only produce stress according to the individual's perception and way of responding to the event. The thought of the Adelaide Crows or West Coast Eagles winning the AFL premiership will produce deep depression and anxiety for many Victorians, euphoria for many west of the Victorian border, and no effect at all for those with no interest in football. It is the same event perceived differently. On a more serious note, two people going through a divorce will respond differently according to their attitude, personality and coping abilities. For one it may be a relief of stress and for the other a trauma. One might learn to let go and move on in life and the other might become fixated on the past and remain bitter for many years. In each case the physiological, endocrine and immune response will react to the perception of the event rather than the event itself. The former person is at minimal increased risk of illness whereas the latter has a much higher risk. A life-event scale, however, may just rate divorce as a stressful life event without taking into account the person's individual response.

The importance of personal characteristics

Early work in PNI showed all sorts of interesting things when it began to map out communication networks between the CNS and immune cells. This went some way to explaining why it was quite easy to classically condition immune responses but early PNI research was also plagued by many inconsistent findings. For example, in response to 'standardised stressors' some people have immuno-enhancement and others immuno-suppression. On this basis one could easily conclude that there is no reliable and predictable basis to stress and its effect on the immune system because averaging out its effects across a group will produce little overall result. When, however, researchers also took into account the individual's perception and coping style over an expectant high stress period, like during exams, it was found that those with positive perceptions and coping styles consistently had immuno-enhancement and those with negative perceptions and coping styles consistently had immuno-suppression and were at greater risk of infection.[6] In short, failing to take perception, personality and coping into account obscures an otherwise important finding.

Inconsistent findings in medical research may largely be related to the inherent difficulties of trying to quantify and define these non physical aspects of human existence. If this sort of research is to proceed in a meaningful way it must take account of such factors, otherwise it will add to confusion rather than reducing it.

Patients often describe the cause of their illnesses in a more holistic way than their doctors, who will generally describe causation in more physical terms.[7] After all, patients experience illness holistically. This is why focusing on quality of life is such an important part of therapy and prevention.

Asking patients about their quality of life turned out to be one of the most powerful ways of predicting how long they would live. The prediction turned out to be independent of anything else we had measured about patients.

Assoc Prof Alan Coates — Royal Prince Alfred
Department of Cancer Medicine, Melbourne

Developing a positive view of life

Psychological state is one, albeit central, factor interacting with many others, such as lifestyle, diet, genetics and environment. Acknowledging psychological factors can make one more able to respond to them, and this can be empowering so long as one diffuses the tendency for the self blame and criticism that sometimes accompanies the recognition of them.

There is much that the GP can do to help patients in this way, whether they have cancer or not. One way is to gently challenge a person's negative perceptions of adverse life events and help them see them in a larger and more positive light. In this way they can produce unexpected benefits, especially if they are measured in terms of self growth and understanding.

This is indeed what many cognitive approaches aim to do. One can enhance positive coping strategies such as:

- improving self awareness
- taking one step at a time
- living in the present
- improving communication
- educating and improving appropriate help seeking behaviour
- learning relaxation and meditation.

One can also minimise the negative strategies like catastrophising, shutting off, inappropriately expressing anger, and avoidance. Whether for prevention of cancer and heart disease, improving quality of life or for survival, such strategies seem to have an important role.[8] One of the most wanted side effects of such enhanced awareness and understanding of the human condition, however, may be the benefits that it confers upon ourselves as doctors and our own ability to cope.

Depression in the new millennium

Dispirited or spiritual deprivation?*

If data in the latter part of the 20th century and projections for the 21st century are accurate then there seems to be a widespread decline in mental health. This phenomenon may be, and probably is, related to a number of factors one of which is be a parallel rise in materialism and body-consciousness. The increasing incidence of mental illness reflects both an increased recognition and an absolute rise in incidence. In any case it seems that rates of depression are soaring. In 1996 WHO figures suggested that it was expected to be a leading cause of burden of disease[1] and those prophesies seem to be coming true, at least in Australia. Recent figures suggest that depression is now the leading disability burden in this country[2] and one would expect the picture to be similar in other Western countries. Approximately 20% of adults are expected to have a major depressive episode at some time in their lives and among the elderly 16% have persistent symptoms.[3]

Levels of stress, whether real or perceived, in the 'western lifestyle' have gone up by approximately 45% over the last 30 years.[4] Youth suicide rates are particularly alarming[5] and, as hard as it is to estimate, 20% of young people are said to have contemplated suicide over the preceding fortnight.[6]

In keeping with our 'illness focus' in healthcare we are concerned with what makes us sick rather than what keeps us well. The very common risk-factors for depression, youth suicide, substance abuse and violence are well known but less publicised are the 'protective factors' which act like an 'immunisation' against these 'social ills.' The most important of these seem to be 'connectedness',[7] and an oft-neglected subject in medical literature, religiosity.

The above figures seem paradoxical considering that the community is meant to be enjoying unprecedented levels of physical health, relative affluence, technological advancement and social freedoms. But paradoxes abound. For example, suicide rates are generally noted to go down during times of adversity such as during major war and many people who contract cancer, if they take a constructive approach to the problem, are heard to say that it had a beneficial effect on their lives. Although one generally does not court adversity it certainly can bring out the best in us and teach us something about ourselves. As Shakespeare said:

"This is no flattery: these are counsellors
That feelingly persuade me what I am.'
Sweet are the uses of adversity,
Which, like the toad, ugly and venomous,
Wears yet a precious jewel in his head;
And this our life exempt from public haunt
Finds tongues in trees, books in the
running brooks,
Sermons in stones and good in every thing.
I would not change it."

As You Like It: Act 2,sc 1

Such paradoxes are not easy to explain but any superficial assessment of human happiness which simply sees it superficially as only satisfying physical needs and wants would have to be questioned closely. Let us look more deeply at one often under-discussed aspect of human life.

What are spirituality and religiosity?

The terms most often used in the medical literature are 'religious commitment' or 'religiosity'. They generally refer to the "participation in or endorsement of practices, beliefs, attitudes, or sentiments that are associated with an organised community of faith."[8] One can also be "extrinsically religious" in that one may adopt the trappings of being religious in terms of behaviours and attitudes associated with that religion. If one holds a strong level of commitment to these behaviours and attitudes then one is "intrinsically religious". Being "spiritual" generally refers to far harder to define and measure things such as "personal views and behaviours that express a sense of relatedness to the transcendental dimension or to something greater than the self."[9] It can encompass meaning, purpose, connectedness and many other intangible qualities. Obviously religiosity overlaps enormously with spirituality. Furthermore, one could conceive of a person being 'religious' without being 'spiritual' or 'spiritual' without being 'religious' in the way defined above.

People pursue meaning and fulfillment via many paths and there are probably as many paths as there are people. But whatever path one chooses, it is likely that a life based on purely materialistic or self-centredness, all the while ignoring deeper human needs, will not fulfill its intended end. Perhaps we often search for fulfillment in things which cannot provide it? And though the search may be honest, if it is misdirected then disappointment, stress, depression and social conflict may be inevitable sequels of such existential pain whether it be on an individual or societal level.

Spirituality and mental health

For many years science and ethics have tended to become increasingly secular thus neglecting or pathologising religion and spirituality. Freud, for example, saw religion as "a universal obsessional neurosis" and described the mystical experience of unity as a "regression to primary narcissism". Jung on the other hand saw the search for spiritual enlightenment as the central, but often ignored, core of human experience. This was one of the main reasons that these two pioneers of psychology parted company. The observation that Freudian psychoanalysis is associated with negative effects on people's health may, however, throw into question Freud's understanding of human nature and may go some way towards vindicating Jung's.[10] Perhaps a simple distinction between Freud's and a spiritual view of the human being is that Freud might have suggested we are base at our core and only think ourselves divine whereas the spiritual view sees us as divine and good at our core but we habitually think and behave in base ways. In any case many of Freud's attitudes have deeply etched their way into psychiatric theory and practice.

"Mainstream psychiatry in its theory, research and practice, as well as its diagnostic classification system, has tended to either ignore or pathologise the religious and spiritual issues that clients bring into treatment."[11]

Undoubtedly human beings for the most part live and think in complex and contradictory ways. We have a subconscious we know little about and have many basic drives which we share with other members of the animal kingdom. The way out of this many would suggest is to become more self-aware, to unravel the complicated knots which lie in the subconscious, and to harmonise the warring factions within our nature. Freud undoubtedly recognised the importance of the subconscious and the influence that basic drives and appetites play but it would be incorrect to attribute to him the 'discovery' of the unconscious. In all great philosophies the realm of the subconscious has been referred to in metaphor and allegory such as Plato's 'underground den' described in book seven of

The *Republic*. Often out of fashion terms like 'living in darkness' or 'being blind' carry a strong sense of the extent to which we are unaware of ourselves and our deeply held thoughts, fears and motivations.

Unfortunately the negative attitude in much of contemporary medicine and psychiatry is out of keeping with the weight of medical evidence which clearly shows that religiosity has a beneficial effect on the mental and physical health of the vast majority of people.[12] The findings were consistent across studies which followed people over time (i.e. prospective) or looked back in time (i.e. retrospective), or whether the study controlled for other lifestyle and socioeconomic factors or not, or whether they looked at prevention of, coping with or recovery from illness.

The effects look to be quite significant as shown by recent data. A population study over 9 years showed that all-cause mortality was significantly reduced and life expectancy increased for regular churchgoers. Life expectancy was 75 years for non-church attenders, 79 years for those who attended less than once per week and 82 years for those who attended at least once per week. Again, the findings were not explainable by the accepted lifestyle and social variables.[13] This is consistent with other data.[14]

In terms of mental health many studies have linked lack of religiosity to depression. Religious commitment is associated with a reduced incidence of depression,[15] and a significantly quicker recovery from depressive illness for the elderly.[16] These findings are not isolated. Two separate reviews of the literature showed similar findings. One demonstrated that people with "high levels of "religious involvement", "religious salience" and "intrinsic religious motivation" are all at reduced risk of depression.[17] The other review showed that religious commitment was inversely related to suicide risk with 13 of the 16 studies reviewed.[18] The increase in risk for suicide is quite large with one study showing a fourfold increase for non-churchgoers compared to regular attenders.[19] No study showed an increased risk.

Other data suggests that religiosity protects against drug and alcohol abuse, one of the most maladaptive and commonly used ways for dealing with depression and other psychological problems. For example, one study showed that 89% of alcoholics lost interest in religious issues in their teenage years whereas only 20% lost interest in the control group.[20] There have also been studies on doctors, who are a high-risk group for substance abuse. Again, religious commitment while in medical school was protective against development of an alcohol problem in later years.[21] Among those with religious affiliation even where alcohol abuse developed it was less likely to be heavy and associated with the clinical and social consequences.

There might be a number of associated reasons why people with a sense of religious commitment are protected against these personal and social ills. It may be that it is the social interaction which protects, the messages about healthy living which often go hand in hand with churchgoing, or perhaps the reduced exposure to drug-taking behaviour in some social circles. All of these would be plausible explanations and probably play an important part however many of the above-mentioned studies tried to control for these factors and still found that religiosity was an independently protective factor. Therefore, there may be other reasons for the observation such as the comfort which comes from having a view of the universe as being governed by a benevolent and caring God, the view that in the end justice always prevails or that adverse events always have a meaning and a message. Such attitudes would buffer enormously against the ill effects of life-stresses and the depression which often follows.

The significant role that mental health plays in the development and progression of many physical illnesses may go part way to explaining why religious commitment is associated with reduced risk for hypertension, heart disease and cancer.[22,23,24,25] Examples of the negative effects of religion are generally more newsworthy in the medical and general press than the positive ones, sometimes, of course, for good reason. This, however, may not be an argument against religion or spirituality but perhaps an argument against blind faith unsupported by reason and effective action.

Relevance to clinical medicine

Gauging a patient's spiritual awareness and/or sense of meaning in their life, at very least, should form an important part of a thorough history. One cannot really be said to know another without an understanding of their responses to the most important questions that human beings ask themselves. Approaching treatment of especially sensitive areas like depression, not to mention terminal illness, will of necessity take place in the dark unless one gauges the response to such existential questions. However, broaching issues around spirituality obviously requires considerable sensitivity, cultural tolerance and the ability to be non-dogmatic. Gently encouraging patients to consider these issues is, in some quarters, becoming a part of contemporary counselling and psychotherapy.[26] Each person needs to explore these issues in a way which suits them. Even if we are not religious ourselves, we may still need to ask important questions about how our colleagues, kin, students and patients find meaning in their lives in a way that is respectful and takes care not to push a line of thought, whether it be religious or secular. Religious sensitivities and biases, like political ones, can make discussion about these subjects difficult.

More in-depth questions about spirituality and religion should probably be referred to culturally appropriate 'non-medical experts'. How far, clinically and ethically, a medical practitioner should become involved in the spiritual life of their patients is a difficult question to answer.[27] At present little if any reference is made to these issues in medical education and practice despite the large body of evidence referred to above. A physical factor of similar relevance to physical and mental health would certainly not be ignored as religiosity and spirituality have been. It is therefore reasonable for medical students and practitioners to be aware of this field of evidence so that they can provide a more holistic approach to information giving, counselling, psychotherapy and treatment. Unfortunately, such a perceived lack of holism is a central reason why many look outside the biomedical model for their health care.[28]

For many, especially the young, the search for meaning is becoming a rarer commodity in the bustle of modern material life. It is not that material concerns are not important but perhaps they have been given a central importance which they do not deserve and other less tangible but vital aspects of human existence become increasingly ignored at their expense. Jung's and Plato's exhortations seem more and more relevant the further we go into this present age.

> *"I tell you that virtue comes not from money but that from virtue comes money and every other good."*

> Plato; The Apology

> *"The lack of meaning in life is a soul-sickness whose full extent and full import our age has not yet begun to comprehend."*

> Carl Jung

Perhaps these issues will become increasingly relevant for those in coming generations where the lack of meaning comes at an increasing cost in terms of depression, suicide, anxiety, social isolation and substance abuse. Maybe a return to a spirituality which is not scientifically naïve nor culturally intolerant may be a pre-requisite for the mental and material wellbeing of the healing professions and the community.

Humour

Is it good for you?

Disclaimer
Before embarking on an article reviewing the science of humour and health the author is obliged, I believe, to sound a warning to unwary readers. This warning was summed up by Mark Twain when he said,

> *"Studying humour is like dissecting a frog — you*
> *may know a lot but end up with a dead frog."*

The author will do his best not to kill the frog but if the frog should die then don't say that you were not warned. Furthermore, the publishers accept no legal or moral responsibility for the death or dismemberment of any of their readers' sense of humour.

That humour has a beneficial effect on health has been long recognised. Doctors of old without modern tools for scientific investigation and the accumulated knowledge of many centuries have had to rely on their powers of observation, clinical experience and intuition. Dr Thomas Sydenham, for example, was a famous 17th century physician. He was in little doubt about the benefits of humour when he said:

> *"The arrival of a good clown exercises more*
> *beneficial influence upon the health of a town that*
> *of twenty asses laden with drugs."*

Drug companies, on the other hand, are not likely to agree. This knowledge about the health-giving effects of humour was well established millennia ago and was obvious to those wise sages of times past.

> *"A merry heart doeth good like a medicine but a*
> *broken spirit drieth the bones."*

Proverbs 17:22

As a reliever of stress humour is without compare. We all know the effect of being in a tense personal, domestic or professional situation when someone was able to break the ice with a timely witticism. Of course, sometimes the last thing in the world we wish to do is to laugh when we want nothing more than to be angry and so an untimely joke can be a risk-factor for serious health problems such as broken bones and premature death. But in the case of the well intentioned and well taken joke then the relief is palpable emotionally and physically. Everything which was seized up moments before, such as the blood-flow to the brain and the saliva flow to the mouth, seems to flow again and our brain's nerve cells which seemed to have lost all communication with each other re-established their synaptic connections. This all happens in the blinking of an eye. Such is the miracle of laughter.

Is laughter good for you?

The benefits of laughter seem to go much further than this however. Let us consider the physiology and effects of laughter. We might start by considering which part of the brain registers humour. It has been observed that with damage to the right frontal lobe of the brain it is difficult to appreciate humour or jokes.[1] Poor function of this part of the brain may play a role in conditions with communicative impairment like autism.[2] Whether damage in the right frontal lobe also predisposes one to extreme and debilitating forms of 'political correctness', however, is a research question which remains to be answered. Observing the negative effect that negative emotions play in facilitating constructive change in various social issues has led some authors to argue that positive emotions like humour would be one of the best ways of making progress. One author went as far as to say that such an approach would be useful in advancing "an enlightened and humanistic form of feminism".[3] Maybe a lot more progress would be made in many social battles if they were approached with a lighter touch. After all, a pre-requisite before we can laugh with others is that we see the funny side of our own behaviour first.

Humour as an antidote to stress

Stress is well known to increase levels of stress-hormones ranging from adrenaline to cortisol. In their place they are fine but out of balance they predispose to various illnesses. Just to illustrate, high cortisol associated with depression and chronic stress is an independent risk-factor for osteoporosis. This stress response takes place via a variety of 'endocrine glands' such as the pituitary gland, which secrete the various hormones governing the body's various functions. According to early research there seems to be proof of the obvious, that is, humour helps to reverse these effects of stress by reducing cortisol, adrenaline and other stress hormones in response to 'mirthful laughter'.[5]

Other stress hormones such as cytokines and interleukins are pro-inflammatory. Switching on such hormones in a stressful situation, like when you are being mauled by a tiger, is useful because you are likely to have a lot of wound repairing to do. But think of all the times you have had imaginary arguments in your head with your boss or spouse before you've even met them, or all the times you've had action replays of stressful events in your imagination long after they have gone. Very quickly you notice that you are fighting imaginary tigers all the time. Unhappily these imaginary stresses switch on the stress hormones inappropriately so that they float around the body and get up to 'mischief', like aggravating inflammatory illnesses. This may help to explain the mechanisms behind many a clinical observation such as a recent study finding that stress in the prior week was clearly associated with increased inflammation, pain and disease activity for patients with rheumatoid arthritis.[6] Another inflammatory disease, Systemic Lupus Erythematosis (SLE), is also significantly affected by life stress.[7] It has also been well shown that negative emotions are a significant contributor to asthma severity and frequency.[8] The effect on outcomes can be extreme as one review of childhood asthma deaths showed where conflict between staff, parents and child, recent emotional disturbance, recent grief and loss, or depressive symptoms were all clearly predictive of risk for fatal asthma attacks.[9]

The obvious conclusion, i.e. that humour would help to reverse these effects, has not been fully tested although there are celebrated cases like that of Norman Cousins who managed to 'reverse' his severe form of inflammatory arthritis (ankylosing spondylitis) with humour.[10,11] In his case such was the power of Marx Brothers movies! Mind you, the prospect of watching many hours of continuous Marx Brothers movies will switch on the stress response for many people!

Stress hormones also seem to stimulate growth of rapidly dividing cells like cancer cells almost acting like 'fertiliser'. Other hormones, like melatonin, are associated with positive and calm states of mind and they can help to reverse these effects and even induce the 'suicide' of cancer cells. Therefore it is being increasingly postulated that our approach to cancer has focused far too much on the cancer cells and has ignored "the aberrant signaling on control pathways malignant cells manifest."[12] Said another way, we may be able to switch off disease processes, at least in part, by changing the signals the body is giving to such cancerous cells. Reducing stress hormones[13] and inducing hormones associated with relaxation and positive mood may be part of the reason why stress reduction and psychosocial interventions help in quality of life for cancer patients and may even prolong cancer survival.[14] The opposite hypothesis, that humour and positive affect can reverse these processes and so improve clinical outcomes has a very strong theoretical, intuitive and anecdotal basis but has not been tested nearly enough. Like a new continent waiting to be explored there is much fertile ground for new research but it is certainly promising (*see* Table p.82). As an example humour has been found to raise immunoglobulin levels (immunoglobulins ward off infections) in the breast milk and saliva of breast-feeding mothers and this is associated with a reduced number of URTI's in both mother and infant.[15]

Negative emotions seem to be a predisposing factor for virtually every disease examined. In heart disease hostility and cynical distrust were associated with significantly more rapid development of coronary artery calcification or 'hardening of the arteries' in young adults.[16] Those with greater than average hostility had 2.57 times the chance of having early coronary calcification and 9.56 times the odds of having extremely high calcification scores. The usual risk-factors for heart disease like smoking were, of course, controlled for. We are still awaiting a brave researcher who is willing to risk their life testing the reverse hypothesis by telling a group of hostile 18 to 30 year olds to 'lighten up' so that the effects on their coronary arteries can be measured.

That humour increases life-span may well accord with our intuition and possibly our anecdotal experience. It is hard to find a really old person who does not have a capacity to laugh at themselves and their adversity. We are still awaiting hard evidence although some data does suggest that long survivors tend to rate higher on humour rating scales.[17] However, the methodology for designing a definitive double-blinded randomised cross-over controlled trial examining humour and longevity makes the mind boggle.

It is difficult to determine what lies behind the therapeutic effects of humour in health settings like hospitals. Is it the staff or the patients who are really being helped the most? One study found that showing humorous videos to schizophrenic patients over a period of time was significantly associated with reduced anxiety and depression. Analysis, however, suggest that the positive effects "may be mediated by the effects on the staff of the incidental exposure to humorous films."[18] We know there is such a thing as 'passive smoking' but this may go some way to proving that there is such a thing as 'passive humour'.

It is also interesting to note that there is plenty of research about humour in medical and nursing journals. There is less literature in the medical journals than the nursing journals about using humour in clinical and educational settings.[19,20] It would seem that nurses may be more ready to laugh at themselves and with their patients than doctors are. Do we, as doctors, take ourselves too seriously? Patch Adams certainly doesn't.

> *"The most revolutionary act you can commit in today's society is to be publicly happy."*

Dr Patch Adams

Conclusion

So who knows, maybe we need to be a little more radical in health care. Perhaps the stethoscope will be replaced by a red nose, the script pad will give way to the joke book, and there will be new subjects in undergraduate medical courses like 'Advanced Clowning'. Maybe we need such a revolution in politics more than we need it in health care. Maybe you think there are enough doctors and politicians who are clowns already.

Nevertheless, you would think that people would be happy to just accept that humour benefits physical and psychological functioning. But no! There are clinical and ethical questions which still need to be answered. Should one try to make people laugh who don't want to? Will informed consent need to be sought before we tell a joke? Will such premeditation 'kill the frog' by quashing spontaneity? What are the indications and contraindications for using humour? Does it have negative side-effects? What are the costs involved? Can you overdose on it? Will it interact with my medications? Considering the economic and marketing potential of laughter, can you distill out the biologically active agent and patent it? Can humour be privatised?

Until such questions are answered health authorities are bound to give only cautious approval to the use of humour in medical settings. Therefore, if you wish to use humour as an alternative therapy or perhaps as an adjunct to your present medical treatment then try just a little chortling. If you tolerate that well enough then try a little guffawing but only under close supervision. Hilarity, however, is not recommended and if your sides should split then please seek medical attention immediately.

Therapeutic effects of laughter: psychological

- Moderates stress and buffers physical effects of stress[21]
- Improves mood, coping with sadness[22,23] and loss[24]
- Adjunct to psychotherapy[25]
- Reduces anxiety and improves performance[26] and teamwork[27]
- Enhances education[28] and occupational therapy[29]
- Coping with terminal illness,[30] hospitalisation and major medical procedures[31]
- Positively associated with creativity,[32] generativity,[33] emotional stability, extraversion[34] optimism and self-esteem and negatively with distress and depression[35]

Therapeutic effects of laughter: physiological

- Longevity
- Reduces pain and improves pain threshold[36,37,38]
- Enhances relaxation response[39]
- Reduces stress hormones, e.g. cortisol[40]
- Improves immunity
- Stimulates IgA[41]
- Increases blood leukocytes[42]
- Reduces stress hormones[43] and buffers against the immunosuppressive effects of stress[44,45,46]
- Improves blood and lymph flow, increases oxygenation, lowers blood pressure and exercises muscles[47]

Medicine

What has love got to do with it?

Is nothing sacred? Investigating the nature and effects of love has always been the domain of theologians, poets and philosophers but now scientists are taking a close look at this most sacred of human emotions.

Biochemical changes

It has been well known for some time that emotional states like depression and anxiety have specific biochemical correlates but it is now becoming obvious that patterns are also recognisable with other emotional states such as love. For example, people in that state of romantic love, (often associated with infatuation and obsession), have high dopamine and norepinephrine levels associated with arousal and low serotonin receptor levels associated with depression, which are very similar to the changes seen in obsessive compulsive disorder (OCD).[1,2] Anyone who has felt the ups and downs of sleepless nights and dark brooding days, especially early in a new romance, can relate to such observations. It has been found that many of these changes revert to 'normal' after the initial stages of romantic love settle down.

States of love

If romantic love is associated with depression is it therefore an unhealthy aberration of an otherwise healthy state of mind? Perhaps not. Language does not serve us well in all cases, for we often use the same word to communicate many and varied states of mind and emotion. Love is defined in various ways from the most superficial and fleeting of human experiences to the deepest and most lasting.

One way of understanding love is as desire, (ie. something which attracts or draws together). It leads the lover to wish to be at one with the object of love, the beloved, whoever or whatever that may be. When together there is fulfilment and happiness but separation causes pain, frustration, anger, loss and grief.

True love, passion and attachment

Love's most common association these days in popular culture might be with the more physical aspects of union. In days gone by this might have been termed 'lust'. Such words have passed from common usage but the phenomenon hasn't.

A more subtle but still common notion of love is that it is a form of obsession or compulsion. Here the attraction is so great that the person cannot bear to be away from the beloved. The lover's thoughts go back to the beloved so regularly that it can consume hours each day and the pangs of separation are severe. Love, in this sense can be compared to an emotional roller coaster ride where our happiness or lack of it becomes inextricably linked with and dependent on the beloved object; in a sense we become owned by it. It is not too difficult to see that when our happiness is on the line in such a way possessiveness and manipulation are quite natural corollaries. The chemical changes with this sort of love, as previously mentioned, resemble those associated with excitation, depression, OCD and addiction. Most of our popular images of romantic love fit this sort of description with the lover experiencing periods of passion and adulation punctuated by periods of insecurity, fear, pining, misery and inability to function. The consequences to this sort of love often make themselves known when relationships break up.

The least common and sensational notion of love is as something steady, peaceful, contented, free and enduring. We sometimes call it Platonic love. It is a love which is not so much of a physical attraction nor is it as prone to the ups and downs of desires and passions like other sorts of love. This type of love does not preclude passion but is not governed by it. This love transcends physical beauty, likes, hurts and dislikes and is the sort of love of which Shakespeare often spoke in his plays and sonnets.

> Let me not to the marriage of true minds
> Admit impediments. Love is not love
> which alters when it alteration finds,
> Or bends with the remover to remove.
> Oh no! It is an ever fixed mark,
> That looks on tempests and is never shaken.
> It is the star to every wand'ring bark,
> Whose worth's unknown although his be taken.
> Love's not Time's fool though rosy lips and cheeks,
> Within his bending sickle's compass come.
> Love alters not with his brief hours and weeks,
> But bears it out even to the edge of doom.
> If this be error, and upon me proved,
> I never writ nor no man ever loved.[3]

Relevance for medical practice

Having taken such an apparently abstracted philosophical diversion, is there a link to more pragmatic and medically relevant concerns? It would seem there are. The relevance of these mental processes, behaviours and biochemical changes are inextricably linked and far reaching, encompassing everything from coping with the effects of broken romance to trying to make healthy lifestyle changes.

Obviously we associate love with the attraction of one human being to another but it can be directed to other things. The link between smoking cessation, depression and obsessional thought patterns is well established.[4] Smokers suffer a similar emotional, psychological and physiological state as bereaved lovers and this is strongly associated with relapse.[5] Hence it is not surprising that concurrently providing cognitive behavioural interventions[6] or treating depression in the process of smoking cessation is associated with better quit rates and less compensatory behaviour such as overeating.[7] Such behaviours are no doubt an emotional and biochemical compensation for the grief associated with the loss.

An addiction to an unhealthy behaviour is almost like a love–hate relationship with an abusive lover where the strong attachment, mental pictures, memories and obsession leads one to continually return to something that we know is not good for us.

Perhaps another sobering and important thing to ponder is raised by the ever increasing levels of depression among our young. People who casts their minds back to their adolescence or are involved in counselling adolescents, will acknowledge that one of the greatest sources of emotional distress involves prematurely getting out of our depth in relationships when emotional maturity and stage of life would perhaps suggest a more cautious approach. Images of love, sex and romance in popular culture may often present the more alluring and seductive but superficial notions of love without the knowledge that extreme highs and lows are temporary and eventually end.

Perhaps, as doctors and counsellors, we need to reflect more on love. A challenge facing all of us, and especially the youth of today, is to learn not so much how to love strongly and passionately but how to also love wisely and prudently. In so doing we may enjoy many of the joys of love without so many of the pains.

Heart and soul

*Thou hast embarked, thou hast made a voyage ...
To be a slave to the vessel (the body), which is as
much inferior as that which serves it is
superior (the mind).*

Marcus Aurelius — Meditations

To many in the medical fraternity the relationship between psyche, social factors and coronary heart disease (CHD) is contentious but for many lay people there is an obvious connection between them. The National Heart Foundation, for example, makes no mention in its promotional literature of any relationship between psychosocial factors and the aetiology or progression of CHD, although it has recently mentioned managing stress as important for quality of life in cardiac rehabilitation. On the other hand, patients may state that when they get anxious or angry, say over a domestic dispute, they 'feel' their blood pressure go up. They notice a range of emotional and physiological changes that intuitively do not feel conducive to good health. They conclude that stress, depression, work pressures, disharmony in social relationships etc. play an important role in illness causation and progression but the lay person's 'evidence' is their experience and intuition.

Feelings and cardiovascular disease

With regard to the evidence for a relationship between psychosocial factors and CHD one recent editorial in the *Medical Journal of Australia* concluded that, 'the identification and treatment of mood disorders, including anxiety and depression, is important for improving quality of life and for reducing the risk of CHD events and mortality.'[1]

A much larger review[2] of the medical literature found that the evidence was very strong, particularly for depression and anxiety having a role in CHD aetiology with 11 out of 11 studies proving positive even when controlling for other risk factors. The relationship was less well defined but still positive for the type-A personality (hard driving, competitive, hostile, impatient), work characteristics and social support. The role of depression and anxiety and social support in the progression of CHD is also very strong with six out of six studies being positive. An even larger review[3] also made a clear statement about the relationship between social factors, mind and heart. Their conclusion was that: 'Recent studies provide clear and convincing evidence that psychosocial factors contribute significantly to the pathogenesis and expression of coronary artery disease (CAD).' They related CAD risk to five specific psychosocial domains, which were: depression; anxiety; personality factors and character traits; social isolation; and chronic life stress.

A meta analysis[4] of 23 studies examining the effect of psychosocial interventions on the progression of CAD found that the increased risk for those with no psychosocial treatment as a part of their management was 1.70 for mortality and 1.84 for recurrence. The conclusions drawn from this study were unambiguous:

'The addition of psychosocial treatments to standard cardiac rehabilitation regimens reduces mortality and morbidity, psychological distress, and some biological risk factors ... It is recommended to include routinely psychosocial treatment components in cardiac rehabilitation.'

Specific mental health problems

Consider some of the specific findings of the studies. Higher anxiety levels were associated with 4.9 times the rate of complications.[5] Another study with 32 years follow up[6] showed that men reporting two or more anxiety symptoms had an increased risk of 1.9 for fatal CHD and 4.5 for sudden death. Previously it had been shown that the increased risk is 3.0 for cardiac deaths in men with phobic anxiety and a 6.1 increased risk for sudden death.[7] Even high levels of 'worry', as opposed to 'anxiety' is associated with 2.4 times the risk of nonfatal acute myocardial infarction (AMI) over 20 years.[8] The studies don't question the relationship between mental health and CHD, but rather they measure and classify the relationship.

Depression is a particular problem, especially following an AMI where the risk of death in the subsequent 18 months is 6.6–7.8 times as great depending on which rating scale was used.[9]

Other important factors

'Vital exhaustion' can be assessed by statements such as: 'At the end of the day I am completely exhausted mentally and physically.' Post-AMI is also a major risk for further complications. When followed for 18 months after an angioplasty, the odds ratio for a new cardiac event was 3.1 for those with vital exhaustion unrelated to the medical condition.[10] Long term follow up of males who complained of exhaustion showed an increased risk of cardiac death.[11]

There is a similar increased risk for stroke especially in men. Those with anxiety and panic are more than twice as likely to die from CHD or stroke.[12] Another study concluded that 'rates of stroke were 2.3 to 2.7 times higher in most subgroups with depressive symptomatology.'[13] Stroke also seems to be related to levels of anger, especially for men, but only for 'outwardly expressed' anger not for 'controlled anger'. Men who expressed more anger had double the chance of having a stroke, whereas the risk grew to 6.9 times as great for men with a previous history of ischaemic heart disease.[14]

There are so called exceptions to the rule according to the findings from some studies[15,16] where psychosocial interventions produced no reduction in mortality for depressed and/or anxious patients who had CHD. What was notable, however, was that in each study the intervention produced no change in depression or anxiety. Obviously an intervention must not only be given but it must also be effective to produce an effect.

From the accumulating evidence it seems that psychosocial factors may contribute to the development and promotion of CHD in some basic ways:

- by promoting pathogenesis of atherosclerosis
- contributing to maintenance of unhealthy lifestyle behaviours, such as smoking and a poor diet
- coexisting psychosocial stresses form a barrier to successful modification of lifestyle behaviours
- direct pathophysiological mechanisms like neuroendocrine and platelet activation.

It should be noted that the treatment of depression with tricyclic antidepressants was associated with a 2.2 increased risk of AMI over 4.5 years. The SSRIs were not associated with an increased risk.[17]

Conclusion

Perhaps some of our time and resources in the management of CHD are misplaced because we concentrate too much on physical factors and do not appreciate enough the relationship of mind and body. Traditionally, in East and West, this relationship has been described as being similar to the relationship between a vehicle and the driver.

Self rides in the chariot of the body,
Intellect the firm-footed charioteer,
Discursive mind the reins,
desire the horses,
Objects of desire the roads.

The Upanishads

It is a well known fact among car mechanics that different drivers get different lifespans out of their cars depending on how they drive them. Some drive hard so that tyres, parts and engines wear out quickly, and some drive carefully and get long mileage out of them. Although a human being is much more than a machine, nevertheless a similar principle may apply.

So what can we glean from the medical literature and philosophical principle? It may be that treating CHD with surgical and pharmacological remedies and yet ignoring psychosocial aspects is like panel beating a car, installing air bags, changing parts etc. but never educating the driver who has such a pivotal role in the causation of the problems. To ignore the driver can be unnecessarily expensive, invasive, painful and ineffective. It may also be that suitably trained healthcare professionals can provide psychosocial interventions for individuals or, more importantly, for groups of patients with CHD such that 'driver education' may be the way of the future.

Connectedness

The social factor and health

From earliest times people have searched for harmony both internally and externally. The word harmony is derived from a Greek word, 'harmos' which means 'to join', suggesting that harmony is a joining of different elements to make a unified whole.

The enjoyable effects of harmony and the unpleasant effects of disharmony are as obvious when we listen to music as they are when we experience health or illness. This need for harmony applies not only for its physical effects, but, more importantly, it may be the need for harmony in our social and family relationships.

Harmony by another name

In more recent times, however, similar concepts go by different names and one that is often used in sociological and epidemiological research is 'connectedness'. Just as disharmony of the body is painful so too is disharmony of social relationships. So painful in fact that the grief associated with the loss of a family member, marital breakdown and conflict at work are among the most stressful things in our lives.[1] The pain of disconnectedness may be expressed in many ways including depression, substance abuse and domestic violence. It is interesting to note that in the context of domestic and social disharmony there appear new philosophies and theories such as 'deconstructionism', 'the selfish gene' and 'chaos theory' which pervade art, music, biology and physics as much as they pervade social theory.

Connectedness and illness

The pain of disconnectedness could encompass a wide variety of experiences from feeling lonely at a party, being ostracised by a peer group, to the breakdown of a family unit. Thankfully such experiences are often transient. Although as doctors we all learn to take a 'social history' in medical school perhaps we underestimate the importance of social connectedness as a causal factor in many of the problems we are required to deal with.

Australia, like many Westernised countries, is trying to cope with a swelling tide of 'social ills' such as high rates of drug use, crime, depression, anxiety and youth suicide. This last problem is on a sharp increase in Australia with suicide rates for the 15–24 and 25–34 year old age groups having trebled and doubled respectively in the past 30 years.[2]

Social isolation and socioeconomic factors are just as significant risk factors as physical indices in some physical illnesses (such as coronary heart disease).[3,4] Furthermore, social factors such as being married, having contact with family and friends, group affiliation and church membership were found to be protective even when these were controlled for lifestyle factors. The progression of heart disease is significantly effected by social factors. For example, it was found that after an acute myocardial infarction (AMI) men who were socially isolated were three times as likely to die from their heart disease in the following 6 months.[5] The effects are especially significant for the elderly with the risk increasing four-fold post AMI.[6] The results could not be explained by the usual risk factors or access to medical care. Similar findings are seen for other diseases. For example, HIV positive patients who were above the median for stress and below the median for social support were found to be two to three times more likely to progress to AIDS over a 5.5 year period compared to those who had less stress and greater social support.[7]

If lack of social connectedness is a causal factor for many physical, emotional and social problems then the solutions may well lie with social structures, attitudes and community values while those at the 'coal face' try to identify patients at risk and minimise harm. The therapeutic potential of increasing social connectedness is probably greatly underestimated and researched.

In terms of the 'social ills' such as youth suicide much attention has gone towards identifying risk factors. Many of these risk factors overlap so they have an additive or synergistic effect. There has been little attention on the positive or protective factors that help to nullify the effects of the risk factors. Thinking of risk rather than protection in medicine may well be symbolic of our concentration on the illness rather than the wellness model.

Risk factor for suicide

- depression and hopelessness
- guilt
- drug use
- concurrent physical illness
- grief
- abortion
- previous attempts
- living alone
- custody and marital problems
- family history
- absence of religion and meaning
- being male

In one large survey family and school connectedness were shown to be tremendously protective[5] not just against youth suicide and emotional distress but also substance abuse and violence.[8] This held across ethnic and economic groupings. The effect of multiple risk factors in the absence of protective factors increased the risk of suicide, but multiple protective factors reduced the risk to near normal even in the presence of multiple risk factors. In the family the most protective elements were parental presence especially at key times in the day (ie. at waking, after school, at dinner and at bedtime) and shared activities between parents and their children. What happens at home and at school, including access to drugs and guns, has a significant effect on adolescent behaviour.

No doubt such observations are as relevant to doctors as they are to the general population. One of the major stresses for doctors is the pressure that medicine exerts on family life because of time, availability, being on call and many other factors.[9]

Having accumulated the evidence what do we do with it? For example, it is difficult to identify the young people at risk of suicide when the risk factors have become so much a part of the fabric of society. It is estimated that of young people who present to a GP for any reason over 20% will have thought about suicide over the preceding fortnight.[10] There is a delicate balance between letting vulnerable youth slip through the cracks, and being over-reactionary.

Emphasising protection versus risk

Perhaps by focussing too much on risk factors we risk making the mistake of not acknowledging and promoting protective factors. But whose job is it to promote protective factors? Is it the doctor's role to be a champion for community values? Certainly the GP can play a valuable role in a number of areas.

- Raise awareness about the links between social factors and health.
- Encourage people to think more holistically about their wellbeing.

- Provide encouragement and support to people wishing to improve their 'social health'.
- Gain counselling skills to help people with communication, conflict and relationship issues.
- Be aware of local resources and support services, especially for young people, which might be useful.

Conclusion

The trend toward disintegration of community, school and family connectedness is an issue that effects us all personally as well as professionally. The causes of social disharmony appear complex but beneath all this complexity there may be some simple themes. The solutions may be difficult to implement unless they are part of a wider movement from government, which includes support for families, education and social programs that help to build a sense of community. Many of these social problems find their ways into doctors' surgeries and, like 'canaries in the coal mines', a lot of stress felt by doctors may be an indicator of this wider community issue.

Music as medicine

Throughout history music has held a privileged place in the hearts of healers. The Greeks worshipped Apollo who, through playing his lyre, had the power to heal. This theme was also picked up in the Renaissance where Marsilio Ficino, for example, combined the arts of philosopher, writer, priest, physician and musician.

> *'Since the patron of music and the discoverer of*
> *medicine are one and the same, it is hardly*
> *surprising that both arts are often practised by the*
> *same man. In addition, the soul and body are in*
> *harmony with each other by a natural proportion*
> *... Anyone who has learned from the Pythagoreans,*
> *from the Platonists, Mercurius and Aristoxenus,*
> *that the universal soul and body, as well as each*
> *living being, conform to musical proportion.'*[1]

Marsilio Ficino

To Ficino music had the power to heal not just the body but, more importantly, the soul, which was the primary cause of what happens in the body. Thus health and justice were described as a kind of harmony, whereas disease or injustice

Summary of the therapeutic effects of music

- Postoperative relaxation and pain management[8]
- Oncology symptom and pain management[9,10]
- Reducing cardiac reactivity and improving performance among surgeons[11]
- Reducing anxiety[12]
- Effects on markers of physiological stress[13]
- Improved cognitive function in the elderly,[14] young adults[4] and children[15,3]
- Improved mood in the elderly[6]
- Improved mood, cardiac and respiratory function for critically ill patients[17,18]
- EEG changes and reduced cortisol in depressed adolescents[19,20]
- Increased empathy in children[21]
- Enhanced immunity[22]

was a kind of discord or disharmony. And as the individual is a reflection of the universe, these musical and mathematical proportions bound and united all of nature.

Even today music holds a special place in the healing professions. Around the world there is an active network of doctors and researchers engaged in both playing music and studying the medical applications of it. Its uses cross a wide range of medical and non-medical fields, highlighting the fact that many astute 'early explorers' into science and health quite accurately used intuition and direct personal experience as their primary tools of exploration.

The therapeutic potential of music, however, is still to be fully tested. The present data available seems to suggest that music has great potential either as an alternative form of therapy for some conditions or as an adjunct to conventional therapy. It can also be used for symptom control and to help reduce the need for medications such as pain killers and sedatives with their unwanted side effects. Listed above are some of the therapeutic effects of music.

An important question is posed by some of the research. Are all forms of music equally healthy or beneficial? Some data suggest they are not and, as with food, taste or habit may not equate with 'nutritional value'. Indeed, musical tastes are deeply personal. They go to the heart of our identity. Music can both express and help to form attitude and emotion. It often says a lot more about our attitudes, identities and personalities than we may know ourselves. Music is a powerful medium for conveying both emotions and ideas.

> *'Musical training is a more potent instrument*
> *than any other because rhythm and harmony find*
> *their way to the inward places of the soul on*
> *which they mightily fasten.'*[2]

Plato — The Republic

For better or worse, many of the composer's moods and messages can be absorbed, whether it be consciously or unconsciously. How often have we found ourselves singing lyrics that have been burnt into our memories, the theme of which we might not otherwise condone if we consciously thought about it?

Some studies have tried to tease out the effects of different musical types and from the limited data it would seem that not all forms of music have the same effects. It has generally been found that classical music such as Mozart, or slower, more melodious music, have beneficial effects on both mind and body. Mozart's music has been most often associated with enhanced learning, whether it be with young children[3] or undergraduates.[4] This was unrelated to whether this music accorded with their usual musical tastes. Interestingly, for young children music training enhanced spatial–temporal reasoning, whereas an interactive computer program did not.[3] The reasons for such observations are still to be fully explained.

As we would expect, harsher, faster and more aggressive music can have a range of negative physiological and psychological effects, including inducing aggressiveness. For example, fast tempo music will increase assertive behaviour in young children.[5] Furthermore, personality types dispose themselves to corresponding music types. Undergraduates who rated high on scales for 'psychoticism and reactive rebelliousness' were drawn to 'hard/rebellious music videos'[6] whereas those who rated lower on these scales were drawn to 'softer' rock music. 'Grunge' rock music has also been found to be associated with increased hostility, sadness, tension and fatigue and decreased caring, relaxation, mental clarity and vigour.[7]

Of course, advertisers and those wishing to influence social attitudes have long known of music's powerful effects on physiology, psychology and behaviour. For better or for worse, it has been used quite deliberately to this end for many years. It is just as difficult to incite people to aggression with a Gregorian chant or Zen shakuhachi flute as it is to induce a peaceful and contemplative state of mind with a rousing movement from a Wagner opera or heavy metal music. For such reasons, Plato felt that various types of music 'fed' different parts of the soul. Discussing music's role in a number of his dialogues he cited 'good music', however we may define it, as an essential ingredient in a balanced and healthy life as well as education.

What does it mean for us? Perhaps we should be just as careful with the food we feed the mind as we are with the food we prescribe for the body. Maybe asking people about musical interests and the messages embodied in them is a powerful way of getting to know what is going on in the hearts of people and of opening up counselling issues especially for the young. It may also be that we have not yet tapped into this potent but safe form of therapy nearly enough, whether it be as an analgesic, educational aid or antidepressant. We may even see the day that a doctor's prescription might be filled at the music store.

Do no harm

'I will follow that system of regimen which, according to my ability and judgement, I consider for the benefit of my patients, and abstain from whatever is deleterious and mischievous... Into whatever houses I enter, I will go into them for the benefit of the sick, and will abstain from every voluntary act of mischief and corruption.'

Hippocratic Oath

The ethical principles of benefiting patients (beneficence) and doing no harm (non maleficence) are as old as the art of medicine itself. Together with the requirements to preserve human life, respect confidentiality, not become sexually involved with patients and to provide medical education, these precepts form the basis of the Hippocratic Oath.

They also provide doctors with some of our most trying moments in clinical practice. In the following discussion we will consider some of the practical and ethical issues surrounding medical maleficence and beneficence.

Adverse events and clinical practice

In Australian general practices and hospitals adverse events are both common and expensive. In general practice for example 805 incidents were counted in a population of 324 GPs over a 20 month period. Seventy-six percent of these were preventable, 27% had potential for severe harm, 34% predicted long term harm and 51% were related to pharmacological management.[1] In hospital it has been estimated that 16.6% of admissions were associated with iatrogenic causes.[2] Of these 50% were judged to be highly preventable. Further follow up showed that the most common cause of these adverse events was due to 'a complication of, or the failure in, the technical performance of an indicated procedure or operation.'[3] To account for human error the authors suggested that better systems and technical support were needed to aid clinicians. The financial costs of adverse events are put at around $401 million per year which makes them the second most expensive cause of injury, more expensive than road accidents.[4]

One would expect that none of us would remain untouched by such events at some stage in our clinical lives. It would seem that as technology and pharmacology become more sophisticated and widely used the potential for such events will only become more likely.

The regrettable cost of such events can be measured in many ways such as physical disability or death, the financial costs and also the emotional costs for the patient, their family and the treating doctor. There would be very few things that could cause as much distress for a doctor as harming a patient — especially when it was preventable. It goes against our human nature as much as it goes against our code of ethics. The residual effects can last for many years and these have been the reason for many doctors ceasing to perform certain procedures, leaving branches of medicine and even leaving the profession altogether. Many questions are posed by these figures, such as:

* Has medicine become overly sophisticated and interventionist?

- Is it understandable that increasing numbers of people look outside the medical system for health care?
- Should the potential for human error be taken more into account when framing medical protocols and systems?
- Do we pathologise and treat too many conditions unnecessarily?
- Have we done enough cost–benefit analysis to see whether the net effect of many interventions warrants their use?
- Do we always prescribe with clear indications in mind rather than to suit patient expectations or feel like we are doing something?
- Do we need to be more aware of safe and efficacious alternatives?

Many of the above issues will be dealt with by improving education standards, supervision, systems and research. There is, however, another more subtle and often forgotten factor when considering beneficence and non maleficence.

The search for goodness

Most of us seek what we see as good and try to avoid what we see as bad. Even in an argument over contemporary ethical issues both sides are still arguing for the same thing, that is, what they believe is right, true and good. This premise could also be extended to someone who is being very devious and dishonest as they may still be trying to attain something they perceive to be of benefit to themselves or others albeit at considerable cost. It would seem that a universal principle is that all people are trying to attain 'the good' but the rub is each individual differs in their perceived notions of goodness and how it might be attained. The oft quoted case of the Jehovah's witness who refuses a blood transfusion will generally be perceived by the medical profession as taking a course of action that is harmful to themselves whereas the patient may feel that the physical harm is worth little compared to the spiritual harm that would ensue if they proceeded with the transfusion. This case illustrates the point that we calculate benefits and harms on different levels and have different priorities.

In the situation of an unwanted pregnancy, two women may see the potential harms and benefits quite differently as may their treating doctors. Deciding on a course of action may rely on a calculation of benefits and harms or on a principle like 'do not take human life'. These calculations are hard to make and until we develop unwavering foresight will always be fraught with uncertainty. Two meta analyses on abortion undertaken at the same time demonstrated this.[5,6] The evidence and conclusions are ambiguous with one saying it does no good and the other that it does no harm. Its associations with a three-fold increased risk of suicide[7] as well as higher rates of ectopic pregnancy,[8] probably breast carcinoma[9] and other problems should give us reason to counsel with great care.

Seeking agreement

Causal relationships between actions and outcomes are often hard to draw because they can be influenced by so many factors. Either more research has to be performed in the field or the debates are pursued with so much passion that objectivity, impartiality and reason are impaired. In any case, we need to be well informed because an uninformed doctor generally means an uninformed patient and the risk of unintended harm becomes far greater. The catalogue of medical history is littered with instances where standard and accepted practices have been found to be far more harmful than beneficial.

Coming back to the principle, however, what we can say is that though we may recommend different courses of action we remain very concerned with preserving beneficence and non maleficence. So although there is apparent conflict between people of differing views there is in fact a lot that each have in common. At least starting from that point of agreement might be enough to help many such discussions proceed in a cooperative and conciliatory way.

Some would suggest that such decisions regarding benefit and harm should be left up to the patient themselves with only information given by the doctor, and by and large that is a reasonable suggestion. But does that solve the ethical and practical dilemmas? Even then the issue can get complicated. Have we not all noticed how we often want things that are harmful and not in our best interests. Have we ever wished to avoid things that are beneficial? We can avoid exercise, telling the truth or going to the doctor though it might do us good. We can overeat or drink, spend and gamble too much, or get angry though it harms ourselves or others. Such actions are clearly not based on full autonomy or reason but on other less desirable factors such as misinformation, manipulation, compulsion, fear, laziness or habit. At another time or with a larger view we may well choose differently.

Practical aspects of this debate

What salient lessons can we take from an examination of issues regarding beneficence and non maleficence? A few will be suggested:

- First, if someone seems to be choosing to be harmed or to avoid vital help then we need to examine our own and the other person's view with great care. Who willingly, consciously and knowingly chooses to be harmed?
- Second, we would do well to acknowledge that there are various levels on which we perceive benefits and harms that include physical, social, financial, psychological, moral and spiritual level. We give these levels different priorities. When taking an apparently harmful course of action it is probably based on some deeply held belief, conscious or unconscious, about what will be more beneficial to us on a deeper level.
- Third, it is useful for us to consciously examine our priorities throughout life. Often a crisis forces us to re-examine our priorities.

- Fourth, there is often a difference between what we want and what is good for us, often expressed within and without as a conflict between reason and desire. It is easy for doctors or patients to get it wrong and then the best we can do is learn from our mistakes so that a harm can be turned to some benefit.

Determining and balancing benefits and harms was a hot issue for Hippocrates and it still is for us today.

Balancing rights and duties

'Liberty means responsibility.
That is why most men dread it.'

George Bernard Shaw

A recent case of a young woman who was both hepatitis B and C positive and needed a surgical procedure raised a difficult ethical issue. Despite counselling and reassurance, she insisted that she did not wish the health team, including the surgeon, to be told about her hepatitis status as she felt it negatively affected people's reactions to her.

This issue raises a number of questions:

*   Should the GP break confidentiality and respect the surgeon's right to be told even though it might cause the woman harm and not respect her autonomy?
*   Should the GP respect the patient's right to autonomy, confidentiality and beneficence and not tell?
*   Whose rights are more important?
*   Who does the GP have a greater responsibility towards?
*   Do we have a right to everything we want regardless of our responsibilities to others?

- Do ethical principles conflict, meaning that one party's rights will be respected while the other's are abused?
- Is there another way of looking at the ethical dilemma that resolves the conflict?
- Can rights be wavered and if so for what reasons and for whose benefit?

Is there a way out of such impasses that can be reasonable and fair for all concerned parties?

Looking for a balanced equation

Most ethical debate these days emphasises promoting and enhancing human rights. This is an entirely admirable and desirable thing, yet the more attention that is paid to this issue, the less it seems to be realised. Perhaps we are only looking at half the picture? The other half of which is a consideration of human duties. The claim to a right to health care, education, work etc, can only be fulfilled by those around us with the required skills, technology and resources to supply the need. Put differently, any right we have is fulfilled by others giving us our dues, that is, honouring a duty owed to us. It naturally follows that if we neglect our duty then other's rights will inevitably be neglected. Rights do not and cannot exist in a vacuum. Often the neglect of one duty will lead to a chain reaction of other neglects further down the line. Soon everybody begins to suffer as much from the subtle fear and mistrust that follows as from any material harm or neglect. Similarly, if we neglect our duty to others then we may find ourselves forgoing some of the rights we might otherwise have enjoyed.

Having our rights and the accompanying freedoms and benefits is certainly attractive. The accompanying responsibilities and limitations that go with them, however, are not always so attractive.

Weighing the options

It seems like a paradox and an inevitability of living in a community, but it is only by each person giving to others that we have our own needs fulfilled, and it is by taking, regardless of others, that we deprive others and eventually ourselves. These duties to our neighbours, whoever they be, are an inseparable part of living in a society. Less obvious but no less dispensable are the duties we owe, not to others, but to ourselves.

Let us revisit the above case but start by emphasising duties rather than rights. The GP has a duty of care to the patient which, at the very least, is to benefit them physically and psychologically. Furthermore, the GP has a duty not to knowingly put colleagues at risk, just as we would wish not to be put at risk ourselves. Similarly, the patient, like every other member of a community, owes a duty to care for those around them. This includes protecting the GP, surgeon and other health workers who might be put at risk in caring for her.

The health team owes the patient a further duty to treat her with the respect they would like accorded to themselves and not to demean her in any way. If such a duty of respect is ignored then it naturally follows that patients will feel more inclined to hide relevant information from the health team. Even though it is understandable that the patient is fearful, the question remains as to whether this is justification enough for her to neglect her basic duties.

It would seem that our modern infatuation with rights at the neglect of fundamental duties has led to some rather curious and intuitively wrong conclusions being proposed with respect to social responsibility. There have been some well publicised cases in Australia recently that have flown under the banner of freedom of speech. For example, some have advocated and instructed in the 'art' of avoiding breathalysers. This case raised the sensitive issue of censorship but the hard decision that needs to be made is whether what is being censored is harmful or not. Although the right to free speech needs to be strenuously defended it also should not be used as a justification for harming ourselves or others. Surely, doing harm to ourselves or others could never be a right. No doubt this raises the whole issue of what is a benefit and what is a harm which is the subject of another article.

Conclusion

How the fulfilment of human rights might be better realised will always be hotly debated. It is hoped that we might progress further, not by denigrating the importance of human rights, but rather by putting them in perspective. If we are really serious about promoting human rights then it seems the only way to do it is to put human duties first, not last.

Towards a more enlightened view of autonomy

*But if you want people to change their behaviour,
you can't do it with proclamations from the top
down by experts. Experts need to learn a new way
of being an expert, to empower people to
participate in the events that impinge on their life.[1]*

Professor Syme, performed much of the original research into cardiovascular risk factors such as the 'Mr Fit Study' and was recently interviewed for the ABC's program 'Health Report'. He was commenting on the need people have for control and problem solving skills in their lives. It was not just a nice sounding catch-cry. He was pointing to consistent and clear evidence that, independent of all other lifestyle factors, a learned or perceived lack of control is the central factor in the evolution of disease, including coronary heart disease (CHD), cancer and all-cause mortality whereas gaining a greater sense of control was consistently associated with better health outcomes.

This word 'control' has many synonyms, including 'autonomy', which literally means 'self government'. Autonomy is often acknowledged as the single most influential principle in modern medical ethics but its connections to physical illness are rarely considered. Reflecting upon it opens up a lot of questions. Is there a healthy expression of autonomy and an unhealthy one? If self government is to be most useful, then which part of the 'self' should one be governed by?

The sort of control that we most commonly recognise is that uneasy balance between tensions and counter-tensions. We, along with our patients, know what it is like to be ruled by fears, despondency, helplessness, anger, misunderstandings and the like. Often we feel that the more we try to stay in control the more we get caught in a cycle of suppression or over-reaction. This is generally accompanied by stress, anxieties, and conflicts both internal and external. Communication is strained, we procrastinate making decisions or they are made rashly, information is difficult to glean, and often we feel like we are manipulated or we try to manipulate others. Decisions made in this state could hardly be called autonomous using the more enlightened sense of the word.

On the other hand, we may have experienced an easy or calm sort of control. Things happen around us and we respond without over-reacting. If conflict occurs around us we are more likely to assist in its resolution rather than its aggravation. At such times it is also easier to keep things in perspective, utilise resources efficiently, make decisions reasonably, hear input from others, communicate effectively and, in short, govern ourselves in a way that is much more satisfying to ourselves and others. We feel it emotionally and physically. If this second sort of autonomy is so desirable then can it be cultivated? Where does it sit with the paternalism that is often associated with doctoring?

For thousands of years philosophers, such as Plato, have suggested that it is vital to foster this more enlightened form of autonomy, that one is better to be ruled by reason supported by positive emotions like compassion, empathy and courage. This reason is also meant to temper the 'appetites'. This more developed sense of autonomy is associated with harmony of mind, body and environment and is gained through right education. Interestingly, clinical research seems to suggest there is something in what Plato said.

'The just man sets in order his own inner life
(balance between reason, emotion and appetite) and
is his own master ... and is at peace with himself.'[2]

Professor Syme noted that patient education aimed at giving information but ignoring the individual skills in self governance and problem solving was nearly useless in producing behaviour change and better health outcomes.

Eysenck, a noted psychologist from the UK, has done a lot of research on personality characteristics and what he calls 'autonomy training' which is based on cognitive and behavioural strategies to increase self-awareness, enhance appropriate communication and cultivate the ability to relax.[3] With the right support, people who are predisposed to cancer and CHD by their personality types can change to a much more autonomous type and in the process reduce their rates of CHD and cancer when compared with controls. Interestingly, studies performed on psychoanalysis demonstrate that it decreases real autonomy over time and is associated with significantly poorer health outcomes.[4]

Sometimes autonomy is a challenging concept for us as doctors but if there is a more enlightened form of autonomy perhaps there is a more enlightened form of paternalism. Paternalism, which means 'of or like a father', should surely be aimed at educating and empowering those under our care. A more enlightened form of paternalism, more than coexisting with autonomy, is actually aimed at enhancing it. That stronger sort of paternalism which is more authoritarian may have a place but surely is a stop-gap measure until the person's own autonomy is sufficiently operational. That one dimensional view of autonomy which is used as a defence of almost any action under the banner of personal freedom will, I suspect, never help us to resolve clinical or ethical dilemmas, nor is it consistent with the human flourishing. Who knows, if we come to understand these concepts better in our own lives and in society as a whole maybe many of the conflicts and incongruities that presently reign may disappear.

Paternalism

Is it a pejorative term?

There exists today an uneasy tension between the traditional role of the doctor, as an authority figure, and the more modern emphasis on a patient's freedom to choose for themselves. In ethical terminology the conflict exists between the principles of paternalism and autonomy, with paternalism viewed as a necessary evil at best and at worst a blatant form of oppression. Such conflicts between the individual and traditional authority figures are not confined to medicine, of course, and seem to be appearing in law, politics, teaching and elsewhere.

Paternalism has been the basis on which the respected role of the doctor has rested for thousands of years. Can it be all bad? Is the conflict between autonomy and paternalism real, or imagined? Can we really do away with the need for authority figures inherent in relationships of service or do we need to rethink and revitalise the way we use that authority so that it respects the patient and prevents misuse?

Autonomy and paternalism — is there a conflict?

The apparent conflict may be in our understanding and practice of the principles rather than the principles themselves. Even the perception that the doctor and the patient are working towards different goals can be enough to undermine the therapeutic nature of the relationship. Whether these two principles are irreconcilable, or whether they coexist harmoniously, is also an important issue to reflect upon. The 'autonomy movement' has borne some good fruit. It has led to better information giving by doctors and empowerment of patients, enhancing their sense of self-responsibility. We as doctors have become more conscious of the need for informed consent and greater scrutiny of potentially unethical abuses of authority, especially in medical research. Enhanced autonomy can enhance patient satisfaction, improve compliance and engage a patient a lot more actively in their own recovery.

On the other hand there is a serious risk that the autonomy movement could swing too far resulting in serious consequences.

Defining terms

Before we begin to consider these, maybe we should get back to first principles. What does the word 'paternalism' mean? According to the Oxford English Dictionary:

'Paternalism — of or like a father.'

Implicit in the role of father, or parent for that matter, might be the duty of providing for physical needs, education, protection, guidance and encouragement of those under one's care. Also required, hopefully under extreme circumstances, may be the occasional enforcing of discipline, for a just reason, though every parent, I dare say, would rather work with their child's consent than without it. Such duties come with the role, and different facets are appropriate at different times depending on the situation, not withstanding the fact that we may play the role for better or worse sometimes. Traditionally the male figure was associated with positions of authority but what is being considered here is more to do with the qualities appropriate to an authority figure, be it man or woman. The most desirable situation is that the individual governs themselves safely and reasonably, but if this is not possible then control may be exerted from an outside source, for example a doctor or statutory body.

In common ethical usage, however, paternalism has come to be interpreted in a different way to the dictionary definition and only one aspect is pointed to, that of enforcement. With that interpretation a number of things have come to be implied in its meaning and hence it is almost a pejorative term.

'Sometimes one has as a doctor to be paternalistic
to one's patients — that is, do things against their
immediate wishes or without consulting them,
indeed perhaps with a measure of deception, to do
what is in their best interests.[1]

Raanan Gillon

This is a very common but one dimensional view of paternalism and authority. Such definitions seem to carry a lot of incongruities. For example, does this mean that it is possible for the doctor to work for the patient's best interests but that the patient freely chooses to work against their own best interests. This seems a little unreasonable and one would surely have to question the competence either of the doctor or the patient. Perhaps the doctor has miscalculated the patient's interests through not paying full attention to the patient's needs and situation. Maybe the patient is not truly autonomous in the fullest sense of the word and their decision is motivated by fear, misunderstanding, habit or some other factor.

Enhancing patients' autonomy

The respect of a doctor may well come with the knowledge, skills, high ethical standards and beneficence implicit in the doctor's role. Like it or not, as a patient, we are all potentially vulnerable and may have a need of the knowledge, skills and compassion of the doctor. Acknowledging an inequality of knowledge, needs etc. doesn't have to imply disrespect or lack of care but perhaps just recognises that there is an unavoidable relationship of trust and an inevitable power imbalance that needs to be handled with great care. But surely 'parents' are interested in their 'dependents' becoming independent. They educate, encourage and empower them within the safe limits of their present ability to make decisions. Surely the 'paternalistic' doctor, in the broadest sense of the word, is passionately concerned in the development, growth and independence of their patients. Put another way, a more enlightened practice of paternalism is aimed directly at enhancing patient autonomy, not restricting it.

It seems that a one-dimensional view of autonomy taken too far gives rise to many potential dangers and dubious public policies. Freedom of speech, for example, is a vital part of a free, vigorous and healthy society but when that call for freedom becomes a justification for promoting crime and injustice then we have to look closely at what is flying under the banner of freedom. This may be part of the reason why we have to look so carefully at issues like euthanasia. The best way to promote rights, use authority and enhance autonomy may not be what it appears to be on the surface. There may come a time when a more enlightened view of paternalism sits very well with a more enlightened view of autonomy, each protecting the other.

Ends & means

The modern world has a love of classification and segregation that gives rise to many '-isms', 'schisms' and '-ologies'. In the realm of ethics there are similar classifications, namely consequentialism or deontology.

End justifies the means

Consequentialism, of which utilitarianism is the best known variety, refers to a theory suggesting that actions are morally right because of the anticipated consequences they are imagined to produce (ie. 'the end justifies the means'). For example, one anticipated consequence might be to produce 'the greatest happiness for the greatest number.' Therefore, to the consequentialist, acts that some might say are inherently wrong, such as taking human life through euthanasia, can be justified because they bring about desirable consequences and avoid painful ones. Many of our modern harm minimisation strategies such as drug legalisation and advocacy of safe injecting houses are generally justified on consequentialist lines.

Means justify the end

The other main camp is made up of the deontologists who suggest that the 'means justify the ends' (ie. actions are right or

wrong depending upon whether they are consistent with funda-
mental duties, laws, rules or principles).[1] Codes such as the
Hippocratic Oath with its modern day reformulations and the
Ten Commandments are examples of deontological systems.
Such duties, rules or precepts, whether taken on faith or tested
in experience, are generally viewed as right because they are:

- 'God-given',
- in keeping with natural law,
- intuitively right,
- or consistent with reason as one notable moral philosopher
  Immanuel Kant attempted to show when he wrote about
  the 'categorical imperative'.

How does this apply in a medical setting?

As a doctor confronted with a decision that contains an ethical
dimension one could approach the issue in these two ways. A
simple example would be whether or not to 'stretch the truth' on
a medical certificate. Consequentialists might or might not do
this depending on how they weigh up the pros and cons,
whereas deontologists might suggest that telling the truth is a
vital duty that should be maintained at all times even if that
means some personal cost.

Although, on the surface at least, these two ways of ethical
reasoning seem poles apart they may not be mutually exclusive.
Each may have a measure of truth but be deficient without
taking the other into account. Despite the fact that such distinctions between theories can certainly provide many hours of
vigorous debate one still wonders whether such debates further
the cause of clinicians grappling with practical concerns.

Euthanasia — as a hypothetical example

In any case let us take an issue like euthanasia and examine it
from the standpoints of the consequentialists and the deontologists. Deontologists might say that the position of the medical
profession and community for thousands of years has been that

there is an absolute moral prohibition against taking innocent human life and therefore euthanasia should be outlawed. 'But what about war?' consequentialists might reply. 'In such situations one must kill or be killed. And what about the moral precept to prevent suffering, which in some circumstances, means taking a person's life when they are in intractable pain.' To answer the first criticism, deontologists might say that: 'Just as the human body's immune system will kill cancer cells or invading bacteria, it only does this in order to preserve life. Similarly the aim of self defence is not to kill but rather to protect life from death where circumstances leave no alternative.' To answer the second criticism about suffering, deontologists, especially if they have spiritual views of life, might say that: 'One has to define suffering in the broadest possible terms. Physical suffering is one thing but one can transcend physical suffering with mind, emotion and spirit and as such there is far deeper joy, inspiration and freedom to be gained by enduring than by capitulating. Think of the most inspirational characters in history and we shall see that they are people who have endured and conquered. And can you really reassure us that there will not be greater suffering in the life hereafter.'

'That is all very well for you to make such distinctions,' respond the consequentialists: 'But we do not recognise your notion of suffering and transcendence and you should not impose it upon me.' The reply: 'It is you who impose your will on the community, for any laws which are made for one are made for all and many others will be left vulnerable on your account.' Consequentialists might say that: 'A doctor can't have absolutist principles because one has to be practical and pluralist and one has to trade off principles like preserving life in order to reduce suffering.' Deontologists might reply: 'It is precisely because of the practical consequences of euthanasia, such as widespread neglect of supposedly strict guidelines and diminishing quality medical care for those who are vulnerable, that the policy is rejected by large scale inquiries. Furthermore, natural laws do not know cultural boundaries.' On the debate could go.

Teasing out the debate

This hypothetical discussion demonstrates that the consequentialists and deontologists are constantly crossing 'battle lines'. Each group is concerned with preserving principle. The deontologists wish to preserve life and relieve suffering. The consequentialists might have to trade off one or other principle depending on the weight they place on the relative importance of each. Both are concerned about the consequences of their actions in terms of minimising suffering through their chosen course of action but they have different notions about what suffering is and how to minimise it. Deontologists do not necessarily deny the importance of consequences but rather might suggest that by not putting duty or principle first, bad consequences will inevitably follow no matter what calculations we make. Therefore duty must be considered the primary cause of consequences. Consequentialists by the same token must take duty or principle into account in order to make any sort of calculation about what is a desirable outcome.

The differences between people on different sides of the ethical fence often have to do with different notions of the role of the law in nature. One may assert that there are no moral absolutes, whereas others suggest that such moral laws do indeed exist and are no less binding than the laws of gravity and that the consequences of ignoring them are no less painful. A wider discussion of the existence or otherwise of natural law and its role in medicine however, is beyond the scope of our present discussions.

At the end of the day it is an important exercise for us all to stop occasionally and reflect upon the basis of our decision making. Consciously or unconsciously we will be following various trains of thought. Reflective thought supported by unbiased observation and practical evidence make for a much surer footing for us as individual doctors or community policy makers.

Conclusion

Throughout the preceding chapters we have gone on a journey tracking through diverse terrain ranging from philosophy to physiology, from psychology to immunology, and from sociology to spirituality. Some of these frontiers have only just been charted and some have been known about for thousands of years and are, in a sense, a rediscovery of old ground full of buried treasures and ancient wisdom.

As our knowledge advances we find an increasingly intricate web of interrelationships between mind, body, society, environment and spirituality. The journey is more than an academic or intellectual one. Such knowledge, devoid of application and experience, is dry and sterile. Watered, however, with a devoted and sincere search for truth and solutions to the problems and dilemmas which humanity faces the ground becomes lush and fertile. The search is for more than just an understanding of science and nature. It is at the same time a journey into Self.

The science investigating the above mentioned interrelationships is infinite in its complexity although, it seems, the principles underlying them mentioned in the chapters of this book are striking in their simplicity. Such principles include, firstly, that all things are connected. No part of the web of our existence is tugged without effecting every other part. Secondly, there is a non-physical dimension of natural law and intelligence, vastly superior to our own, which underpins, directs and orders the physical world.

"There are more things in heaven and earth,
Horatio, than are dreamt of in your philosophy."

Shakespeare, Hamlet Act 1: sc 5.

An essentially materialistic or physical view of science and the world which ignores this runs the risk of being ineffective and inefficient at best and, at worst, of being harmful and devoid of moral principle. Thus it is always wise to try and answer the philosophical and moral questions regarding the use of medical advances and technology before we try to answer the scientific ones. Do we not try to assure ourselves of the motives and soundness of mind of a person before we put a gun into their hands? Potentially the largest of all such challenges comes with the advent of genetic engineering which potentially opens a larger Pandora's box than we have previously seen before. It does not take long to consider the various ways in which powerful medical scientific knowledge can be squandered and misused whether it be wittingly or unwittingly. The power to do the most good brings with it the power to do the most harm. As the adage goes, "discretion is the better part of valour."

We should be optimistic for the future, however, but to realise this on a practical level, what we may need to do is to appreciate the importance of wise and tried principles in clinical decision making and health policy. Policy-makers could make their implementation more than an optional nicety; rather they could be a practical necessity. For example, hundreds of cardiology centres now run the Ornish program for heart disease in the U.S. largely because patients and insurance companies have supported it. Good quality medical care is entirely consistent with good economics because they run on the same principles. Furthermore, medical education and the health system could train and facilitate motivated doctors in taking groups which provide education and support for patients with conditions as diverse as cancer, auto-immune conditions and stress. This not only provides very cost-effective health care and efficient use of the doctor's time but also avails itself of the many other benefits for patients which flow from group support. These benefits include better mental and physical health and an enhanced capacity to cope with physical illness.

Rather than consider whether we can afford such changes to health care delivery we might better ask ourselves how long we can afford to ignore them. Unfortunately policy has not always been driven by wisdom or evidence and sometimes political expediency wins the day. But what appears expedient in the short term is generally expensive in the longer term. So political wisdom must work along side scientific knowledge if we are ever to advance in a sure and safe way.

Discovering new frontiers in medical science, like any other endeavour, requires a little daring and a lot of flexibility of mind. If our thinking remains limited then we, like those who followed the 'flat-earth' thinking of times past, will never sail beyond the horizons of what we presently see to discover new lands. To us it will appear that the horizon is the limit of the known world and there is nothing beyond. Sir Isaac Newton, like many before and since who took knowledge into new realms, had a strong sense of this vast intelligence of which he was given a glimpse.

"I do not know what I may appear to the world,
but to myself I seem to have been only like a boy
playing on the seashore, and diverting myself in
now and then finding a smoother pebble or a
prettier shell than ordinary, whilst the great ocean
of truth lay all undiscovered before me."

Brewster's Memoirs of Newton II, ch. 27.

Whatever happens, the story of human history, as it passes before our eyes, makes for fascinating reading.

References

KNOWLEDGE AND INTUITION p.1

1. Oxford English Dictionary.
2. Meshberger F. An interpretation of Michelangelo's Creation of Adam based on neuroanatomy. JAMA 1990; 264(14):1837–1841.
3. Ornish D, Brown S, Scherwitz L, et al. Can lifestyle changes reverse coronary heart disease? Lancet 1990; 336:129–133.
4. Gould K, Ornish D, Kirkeeide R, et al. Improved stenosis geometry by quantitative coronary angiography after vigorous risk factor modification. Am J Cardiol 1992; 69(9):845–853.
5. Gould K, Lance M, Ornish D, et al. Changes in myocardiol perfusion abnormalities by positron emission tomography after long–term, intensive risk factor modification. JAMA 1995; 274(11):894–901.
6. Ornish D, Scherwitz L, Billings J, et al. Intensive lifestyle changes for reversal of coronary heart disease. JAMA 1998; 280:2001–2007.
7. Woloshynowych M, Valori R, Salmon P. General practice patient's beliefs about their symptoms. Br J Gen Pract 1998; 48:885–889.

THE BODY IS THE SHADOW OF THE SOUL p.5

1. The letters of Marsilio Ficino. London: Shepheard Walwyn; 1988. Vol 4, letter 51.
2. Shakespeare. Macbeth Act 5, scene 5.
3. Hassed C. Spirituality and health. Aust Fam Physician 1999; 28(4).
4. Watkins A. Mind–body medicine: a clinicians guide to psychoneuroimmunology. New York: Churchill Livingstone, 1997.
5. McEwan B. Protective and damaging effects of stress mediators. N Engl J Med 1998; 338:171–179.
6. Bosma H, Marmot M, Hemigway H, et al. Low job control and risk of coronary heart disease in Whitehall II (prospective cohort) study. Br Med J 1997; 314:558–565.
7. Michelson D, Stratakis C, Hill L, et al. Bone mineral density in women with depression. N Engl J Med 1996; 335(16):117–1181.
8. Harvey I Nelson S, Lyons R, et al. A randomised controlled trial and economic evaluation of counselling in primary care. Brit J Gen Pract 1998; 48(428):1043–1048.
9. Bertakis K, Callahan E, Helms L, et al. Physician practice styles and patient outcomes: differences between family practice and general internal medicine. Medical Care 1998, 36(6):879–891.
10. Hemmings A. Counselling in primary care: a randomised controlled trial. Patient Education Counselling 1997; 32(3):219–230.
11. Plato: Charmides. Britannica Great Books of the Western World. Translated by Benjamin Jowett.

SPIRITUALITY AND HEALTH p.14

1. Matthews D, McCullough M, Larson D, et al. Religious commitment and health status. Arch Fam Med 1998; 7:118–124.
2. Levin J, Vanderpool H. Is frequent religious attendance really conducive to better health? Toward an epidemiology of religion. Soc Sci Med 1987; 24:589–600.
3. Kune G, Kune S, Watson L. Perceived religiousness is protective for colorectal cancer: data from the Melbourne Colorectal Cancer Study. J R Soc Med 1993; 86:645–647.
4. Larson D, Wilson W. The religious life of alcoholics. Southern Medical Journal 1980;73:723–727.
5. Koenig H, George L, Peterson B. Religiosity and remission of depression in medically ill older patients. Am J Psychiatry 1998; 155(4):536–542.

6. Koenig H, et al. Int J Psychiatry Med 1998; 155(4):536–542.
7. Asser S, Swan R. Child fatalities from religion motivated medical neglect. Pediatrics 1998; 101(4):625–629.

WESTERN PSYCHOLOGY MEETS EASTERN PHILOSOPHY p.18
1. His Holiness the Dalai Lama, Cutler H. The art of happiness — a handbook for living. Sydney: Hodder, 1999.
2. Mental Health Foundation Survey, issue 7. Newsletter of the National Mental Health Strategy, Canberra. September 1998; 3
3. Quiles Z, Bybee J. Chronic and predispositional guilt: relations to mental health, prosocial behaviour and religiosity. J Pers Assess 1997; 69(1):104–126.

WHAT IS ORTHODOX MEDICINE? p.23
1. MacLennan A, Green R, O'Shea R, et al. Routine hospital admission in twin pregnancy between 26 and 30 weeks gestation. Lancet 1990; 335(8684):267–269.
2. Andrews W, Leveno K, Sherman M, et al. Elective hospitalisation in the management of twin pregnancy. Obstetrics and Gynaecology 1991;77(6):826–31.
3 Hirst G. Health Report, March 1, 1999: www.abc.net.au/rn
4 Linde K., Clausius N., Ramirez G. et al. Are the clinical effects of homeopathy placebo effects? A meta–analysis of placebo controlled trials. Lancet 1997;350(9081):834–43.
5 Fisher P, Ward A. Complementary medicine in Europe. BMJ 1994;309:107–11.
6 Eskinazi D. Homeopathy re–visited. Is homeopathy compatible with biomedical observations? Archives of Internal Medicine 1999;159(17):1981–7.
7 Meade T, Brennan P. Determination of who may derive most benefit from aspirin in primary prevention. BMJ 2000;321:13–17.
8 MacLennan A., Wilson D., Taylor A. Prevalence and cost of alternative medicine in Australia. Lancet 1996;347(9001):569–73.
9 Astin J. Why patients use alternative medicine: results of a national study. JAMA 1998;279(19):1548–53.
10 Downer S, Cody M, McClusky P. et al. Pursuit and practice of complementary therapies by cancer patients receiving conventional treatment. BMJ 1994;309:86–9.
11 Murray J, Shepherd S. Alternative or additional medicine? A new dilemma for the doctor. Journal of the Royal College of General Practitioners 1988;38:511–4.

THE RISKS AND BENEFITS OF COMPLEMENTARY MEDICINE P.28
1. Hirst G. NHMRC Australian guidelines for the management of prostate disease.
2. Berlowitz D, et al. Inadequate management of blood pressure in a hypertensive population. N Engl J Med 1998; 339:1957–1963.
3. McKinlay J. Physician variability and uncertainty in the management of breast cancer. Med Care 1998; 36:385–389.
4. MacLennan A, Wilson D, Taylor A. Prevalence and cost of alternative medicine in Australia. Lancet 1996; 347(9001):569–573.
5. Commonwealth Department of Health and Family Services. Therapeutic goods administration review. Canberra: Commonwealth Government, 1997.
6. Eisenberg D, Davis R, Ettner S, et al. Trends in alternative medicine use in the United States, 1990–1997: results of a follow–up national survey. JAMA 1998; 280(18):1569–1575.
7. Wetzel M, Eisenberg D, Kaptchuk T. Courses involving complementary and alternative medicine at US medical schools. JAMA 1998; 280(9):784–787.
8. Astin J. Why patients use alternative medicine: results of a national study. JAMA 1998; 279(19):1548–1553.
9. Linde K, Clausius N, Ramirez G, et al. Are the clinical effects of homeopathy placebo effects? A meta–analysis of placebo controlled trials. Lancet 1997; 350(9081):834–843.

10. Murphy M, Donavan S. The physical and psychological effects of meditation: a review of contemporary research with a comprehensive bibliography. Inst Noetic Sci 1997.
11. Watkins A. Mind–body medicine. A clinicians guide to psychoneuroimmunology. Churchill Livingstone, 1997.
12. Verbach et al. Efficacy and tolerability of St John's Wort versus imipramine in patients with severe depressive episodes according to ICD–10. Pharmacopsychiatry 1997; 30:81–5.
* These modalities include mind–body medicine, meditation and relaxation therapies, herbal medicine, nutritional and environmental medicine, homeopathy, chiropractic and osteopathy, acupuncture, traditional Chinese medicine, Ayurveda and many others.
** As far as herbs are concerned we are finding out more all the time. For example the herb, St John's Wort, was as effective as imipramine for depression but had the advantage of fewer side-effects.[12]

CONTEMPLATIVE PRACTICES AND HEALING p.33
1. Astin J. Stress reduction through mindfulness meditation. Effects on psychological symptomatology, sense of control, and spiritual experiences. Psychotherapy and Psychosomatics 1997; 66(2):97–106.
2. Shapiro S, Schwartz G, Bonner G. Effects of mindfulness based stress reduction on medical and premedical students. J Behav Med 1998; 21(6):581–599.

TO BE OR NOT TO BE p.40
1. Castillo-Richmond A, Sneider R, Alexander C, et al. Effects of stress reduction on carotid atherosclerosis in hypertensive African Americans. Stroke 2000; 31:568–573.
2. Kiecolt-Glaser J, Marucha P, Malarkey W,et al. Slowing of wound healing by psychological stress. Lancet 1995; 346:1194–1196.
3. Fischman H, Pero R, Kelly D. Psychogenic stress induces chromosomal and DNA damage. Int J Neurosci 1996; 84(1–4):219–227.
4. Kiecolt–Glaser J, Glaser R. Psychoneuro–immunology and immunotoxicology: implications for carcinogenesis. Psychosom Med 1999; 61(3):271–272.
5. Self D, Nestler E. Relapse to drug seeking: neural and molecular mechanisms. Drug Alcohol Depend 1998; 51(1–2):49–60.
6. Cui Y, Gutstein W, Jabr S, et al. Control of human vascular smooth muscle cell proliferation by sera derived from 'experimentally stressed' individuals. Oncol Reports 1998; 5(6):1471–1474.
7. Lopez J, Chalmers D, Little K, et al. Regulation of serotonin 1A, glucocorticoid, and mineralocorticoid receptor in rat and human hippocampus: implications for the neurobiology of depression. Biol Psychiatry 1998; 43(8):547–573.
8. Benes F. The role of stress and dopamine–GABA interactions in the vulnerability for schizophrenia. J Psychiatr Res 1997; 31(2):257–275.
9. Hassed C. The economy of health. Aust Fam Physician 2000; 29(5):475–476.
10. Orme–Johnson D, Herron R. An innovative approach to reducing medical care utilisation and expenditures. Am J Manag Care 1997; 3:135–144.
11. Syme S L, Balfour J. Explaining inequalities in coronary heart disease. Lancet 1997; 350(9073):231–232.
12. Kesterton J. Metabolic rate, respiratory exchange ratio and apnoeas during meditation. Am J Physiology 1989; 256(3):632–638.
13. Benson H. The relaxation response and norepinephrine: a new study illuminates mechanisms. Aust J Clin Hypnotherapy Hypnosis 1989; 10(2):91–96.
14. Mills P, Schneider R, Hill D, et al. Beta–adrenergic receptor sensitivity in subjects practicing TM. J Psychosom Res 1990; 34(1):29–33.

15. Delmonte M. Physiological responses during meditation and rest. Biofeedback Self Regul 1984; 9(2):181–200.
16. Bagga O, Gandhi A, Bagga S. A study of the effect of TM and yoga on blood glucose, lactic acid, cholesterol and total lipids. J Clin Chem Clin Biochem 1981; 19(8):607–608.
17. Echenhofer F, Coombs M. A brief review of research and controversies in EEG biofeedback and meditation. J Transpersonal Psychology 1987; 19(2):161–171.
18. Deepak K, Manchanda S, Maheshwari M, et al. Meditation improves clinicoelectroencephalographic measures in drug resistant epileptics. Biofeedback Self Regul 1994; 19:(1)25–40.
19. Jevning R, Anand R, Biedebach M, et al. Effects on regional cerebral blood flow of TM. Physiol Behav 1996; 59(3):399–402.
20. Coehlo R, Silva C, Maia A, et al. Bone mineral density and depression: a community study in women. J Psychosom Res 1999; 46(1):29–35.
21. Werner O, Wallace R, Charles B, et al. Long term endocrine changes in subjects practicing the TM and TM–siddhi program. Psychosom Med 1986; 48(1–2):59–65.
22. Reiter R, Robinson J. In: Melatonin. New York, London: Bantam Books, 1995.
23. Brzezinski A. Melatonin in humans. N Engl J Med 1997; 336:186.
24. Kusaka Y, Kondeu H, Marimoto K, et al. Healthy lifestyles are associated with higher natural killer cell activity. Prev Med 1992; 21:602–615.
25. Kiecolt–Glaser J. Psychoneuroimmunology: Can psychological interventions modulate immunity? J Consult Clin Psychol 1992; 60(4):569–575.
26. Kabat–Zinn J. Four year follow up of a meditation based program for the self–regulation of chronic pain; treatment outcomes and compliance. Clin J Pain 1987; 2:159–173.
27. Wilson A, Honsberger R, Chiu J, et al. Transcendental meditation and asthma. Respiration 1975; 32:74–80.
28. Cerpa H. The effects of clinically standardised meditation on type 2 diabetics. Dissertation Abstracts International 1989; 499(8b):3432.
29. Kabat–Zinn J, Massion A, Kristeller J, et al. Effectiveness of a meditation based stress reduction program in the treatment of anxiety disorders. Am J Psychiatry 1992; 149:936–943.
30. Eppley K, Abrams A, Shear J, et al. Differential effects of relaxation techniques on trait anxiety: a meta–analysis. J Clin Psychol 1989; 45(6):957–974.
31. Teasdale J, Segal Z, Williams J. How does cognitive therapy prevent depressive relapse and why should attention control (mindfulness) training help? Behav Res Ther 1995; 33(1):25–39.
32. Bujatti M, Riederer P. Serotonin, noradrenaline, dopamine metabolites in TM technique. J Neural Transm 1976; 39(3):257–267.
33. Alexander C, Rainforth M, Gelderloos P, et al. TM, self actualisation, and psychological health: a conceptual overview and statistical meta–analysis. J Social Behaviour Personality 1991; 6(5):189–248.
34. Kornfield J. Intensive insight meditation: a phenomenonological study. J Transpersonal Psychology 1979; 11(1):48–51.
35. Kutz I, Lerserman J, Dorrington C, et al. Meditation as an adjunct to psychotherapy. An outcome study. Psychother Psychosom 1985; 43(4):209–218.
36. Gelderloos P, Walton K, Orme-Johnson D, et al. Effectiveness of the TM program in preventing and treating substance misuse: a review. Int J Addict 1991; 26:293–325.
37. Mason L, Alexander C, Travis F, et al. Electrophysiological correlates of higher states of consciousness during sleep in long–term practitioners of the TM program. Sleep 1997; 20(2):102–110.

38. Abrams A, Seigel L. The TM program and rehabilitation at Folsom Prison: a cross validation study. Criminal Justice and Behaviour 1978; 5(1):3–20.
39. Carrington P, Collings G, Benson H, et al. The use of meditation and relaxation techniques for the management of stress in a working population. J Occup Med 1980; 22(4):221–231.
40. Jedrczak A, Toomey M, Clements G, et al. The TM–siddhi program, age, and brief tests of perceptual motor speed and nonverbal intelligence. J Clin Psychol 1986; 42(1):161–164.
41. Brown D, Forte M, Dysart M, et al. Visual sensitivity and mindfulness meditation. Percept Mot Skills 1984; 58:775–784.
42. Fiebert M. et al. 'Meditation and academic performance.' Perceptual and Motor Skills 1981; 53(2):447–450.
43. Verma I, Jayashan B, Palani M, et al. Effect of TM on the performance of some cognitive and psychological tests. Int J Med Res 1982; 7:136–143.
44. Delmonte M, Kenny V. Conceptual models and functions of meditation in psychotherapy. J Contem Psychotherapy 1987; 17(1):38–59.

THE ECONOMY OF HEALTH p.45

1. Special edition: New Technology. Med J Aust 1999; (10):171.
2. Victorian Government. Annual Report 1997–1998. www.dhs.vic.gov.au
3. Top ten drugs. Australian Prescriber 1999; 22(5):119
4. Pritchard D, Hyndman J, Taba F. Nutritional counselling in general practice: a cost effective analysis. J Epidemiol Community Health 1999; 53(5):311–316.
5. Baxter T, Milner P, Wilson K, et al. A cost effective, community based heart health promotion project in England: prospective comparative study. Br Med J 1997; 315(7108):582–585.
6. Pelletier K. Clinical and cost outcomes of multifactorial, cardiovascular risk management interventions in worksites: a comprehensive review and analysis. J Occup Environ Med 1997; 39(12):1154–1169.
7. Scientific Advisory Board. Osteoporosis Society of Canada. Clinical practice guidelines for the diagnosis and management of osteoporosis. 1996; 155(8):1113–1129.
8. Coupland C, Cliffe S, Bassey E, et al. Habitual physical activity and bone mineral density in postmenopausal women in England. Int J Epidemiol 1999; 28(2):241–246.
9. Geelhoed E, Harris A, Prince R. Cost–effectiveness analysis of hormone replacement therapy and lifestyle intervention for hip fracture. Aust J Public Health 1994; 18(2):153–160.
10. Kerse N, Flicker L, Jolley D, et al. Improving the health behaviours of elderly people: randomised controlled trial of a general practice education programme. Br Med J 1999; 319:683–687.
11. Anonymous. Promoting health through schools. Report of a WHO Expert Committee on Comprehensive School Health Education and Promotion. WHO Technical Report Series 1997; (I–IV)870:1–93.
12. Hellman C, Budd M, Borysenko J, et al. A study of the effectiveness of two group behavioural medicine interventions for patients with psychosomatic complaints. Behav Med 1990; 16(4):165–173.
13. Orme–Johnson D, Herron R. An innovative approach to reducing medical care utilisation and expenditures. Am J Manag Care 1997; 3:135–144.
14. Ornish D, Brown S, Scherwitz L, et al. Can lifestyle changes reverse coronary heart disease? Lancet 1990; 336:129–133.

15. Ornish D, Scherwitz L, Billings J, et al. Intensive lifestyle changes for reversal of coronary heart disease. JAMA 1998; 280:2001–2007.
16. News. US insurance company covers lifestyle therapy. Br Med J 1993; 307:465.

EVIDENCE — WHOSE EVIDENCE? p.50
1 www.abc.net.au/rn/talks/8.30/helthrpt/stories/s136600.htm
2 Moynihan R, Bero L, Ross-Degnan D. et al. Coverage by the news media of the benefits and risks of medications. New Engl J Med 2000;342(22):1645–50.
3 Bodenheimer T. Uneasy alliance — clinical investigators and the pharmaceutical industry. New Engl J Med 2000;342(20):1539–44.
4 Faculty policies on integrity in science. Cambridge, Mass.: Harvard University, February 1996.

PSYCHONEUROIMMUNOLOGY p.55
1. Ader R, Felten D, Cohen N. Psychoneuroimmunology, 2nd ed. New York: Academic Press, 1991.
2. Watkins A. Mind–body medicine: A clinicians guide to psychoneuroimmunology. London: Churchill Livingstone, 1997.
3. Cohen S, Tyrell D, Smith A. Psychological stress and susceptibility to the common cold. N Eng J Med 1991; 325(9):606–612.
4. Glaser R, Kiecolt-Glaser J, Bonneau R, et al. Stress induced modulation of the immune response to recombinant hepatitis B vaccine. Psychosom Med 1992; 54:22–29.
5. Keicolt-Glaser J, Glaser R, Gravenstein S, et al. Chronic stress alters the immune response to influenza virus vaccine in older adults. Proceedings of the National Academy of Science 1996; 93:3042–3047.
6. Kiecolt-Glaser J, Glaser R. Psycho–neuroimunology: Can psychological interventions modulate immunity? J Conslut Clin Psychol 1992; 60:569–575.
7. Smyth J, Stone A, Hurewitz I, et al. Effects of writing about stressful experiences on symptom reduction in patients with asthma or rheumatoid arthritis. A randomised trial. JAMA 1999; 281:1304–1309.
8. Kusaka Y, Kondou H, Morimoto K, et al. Healthy lifestyles are associated with higher NK cell activity. Prev Med 1992; 21:602–615.
9. Fawzy I, Fawzy N, Hyun C, et al. Malignant melanoma: Effects of an early structured psychiatric intervention, coping and affective state on recurrence and survival after six years. Arch Gen Psychiatry 1993; 50:681–689.
10. Monier-Williams Sanskrit Dictionary.
11. The letters of Marsilio Ficino. London: Shepheard Walwyn; 1988.
12. Resnick M, Bearman P, Blum R, et al. Protecting adolescents from harm. Findings from the National Longitudinal study on Adolescent Health. JAMA 1997; 278(10):823–832.

THE PERSONA AND HEALTH p.60
1. Watkins A (ed). Mind-body Medicine — A clinician's guide to psychoneuroimmunology. Churchill Livingston, 1997.
2. Eysenck H, et al. Creative novation behaviour therapy as a prophylactic treatment for cancer and CHD: Part 2 — Effects of treatment. Behav Res Ther 1991; 29(1):1–31.
3. Kune G, et al. Personality as a risk factor in large bowel cancer. Psychological Medicine 1991; 21:29–41.
4. Blumenthal J, et al. Stress management and exercise training in cardiac patients with myocardial ischaemia. Arch Intern Med 1997; 157:2213–2223.
5. Denollet J, et al. Personality, disease severity and the risk of long-term cardiac events in patients with decreased ejection fraction after myocardial infarction. Circulation 1998; 97:1521–1526.

STRESS AND CANCER p.63

1. Protheroe D, Turvey K, Horgan K, et al. Stressful life events and difficulties and onset of breast cancer: case control study. Br Med J 1999; 319:1027–1030.
2. Watson M, Haviland J, Greer S, et al. Influence of psychological response on survival in breast cancer: a population-based study. Lancet 1999; 354:1331–1336.
3. Chen C, David A, Nunnerley H, et al. Adverse life events and breast cancer: a case control study. Br Med J 1995; 311:1527–1530.
4. Kune S, Kune G, Watson L, et al. Recent life change and large bowel cancer. Data from the Melbourne colorectal cancer study. J Clin Epidemiol 1991; 44:57–68.
5. Evans D, Leserman J, Perkins D, et al. Severe life stress as a predictor of early disease progression in HIV infection. Am J Psychiatry 1997; 154:630–634.
6. Jemmott J, Borysenko J, Borysenko M, et al. Academic stress, power motivation, and decrease in secretion rate of salivary secretory immunoglobulin A. Lancet 1983; 1(8339):1400–1402.
7. Woloshynowych M, Valori R, Salmon P. General Practice patient's beliefs about their symptoms. Br J Gen Pract 1998; 48:885–889.
8. Eysenck H, Grossarth-Maticek R. Creative novation behaviour therapy as a prophylactic treatment for cancer and coronary heart disease: parts 1 & 2. Behav Res Ther 1991; 29(1):1–16,17–31.

DEPRESSION IN THE NEW MILLENNIUM p.68

*   Adapted from Hassed C. Depression: dispirited or spiritually deprived. MJA 2000. In press.
1   Murray C, Lopez A. The global burden of disease. 1996, World Health Organisation.
2   Mathers C, Vos E, Stevenson C, Begg S. The Australian Burden of Disease Study: measuring the loss of health from diseases, injuries and risk factors. MJA 2000;172:592–6.
3   Rey J. The epidemiological catchment area study: implications for Australia. MJA 1992;156:200–3.
4   Miller M, Rahe R. Life changes scaling for the 1990's. J Psychosom Res. 1997;43(3):279–92.
5   Cantor C, Neulinger K, De Leo D. Australian suicide trends 1964–1997: youth and beyond? MJA 1999;171:137–41.
6   McKelvey R, Davies L, Pfaff J et al. Psychological distress and suicidal ideation among 15–24 year olds presenting to a general practice: a pilot study. Australian and New Zealand Journal of Psychiatry 1998;32(3):344–8.
7   Resnick M, Bearman P, Blum R et al. Protecting adolescents from harm; findings from the National Longitudinal Study on Adolescent Health. JAMA 1997;278(10):823–32.
8   Matthews D, McCullough M, Larson D, et al. 'Religious commitment and health status: a review of the research and implications for family medicine.' Archives of Family Medicine 1998;7(2):118–24.
9   Reed P. Spirituality and wellbeing in terminally ill hospitalised patients. Res Nurs Health 1987;9:35–41.
10 Grosarth–Maticek R., Eysenck H. Prophylactic effects of psychoanalysis on cancer prone and coronary heart disease prone probands, as compared with control groups and behaviour therapy groups. Behav Ther Exp Psychiatry 1990;21(2):91–9.
11 Lukoff D, Fu F, Turner R. Cultural considerations in the assessment and treatment of religious and spiritual problems. Psychiatry Clin North Am 1995;18(3):467–85.
12 Matthews D, McCullough M, Larson D, et al. 'Religious commitment and health status: a review of the research and implications for family medicine.' Arch Fam Med 1998;7(2):118–24.
13 Hummer R., Rogers R., Nam C. et al. Religious involvement and U.S. adult mortality. Demography 1999;36(2):273–85.

14 Clark K., Friedman H., Martin L. A longitudinal study of religiosity and mortality risk. Journal of Health Psychology 1999;4(3):381–91.
15 Gartner J., Larson D., Allen G. Religious commitment and mental health: a review of the empirical literature. J Psychol Theol 1991;19:6–25.
16 Koenig H., George L., Perterson B. Religiosity and remission of depression in medically ill older patients. American Journal of Psychiatry 1998;155:536–42.
17 McCullough M, Larson D. Religion and depression: a review of the literature. Twin Research 1999;2(2):126–36.
18 Gartner J, Larson D, Allen G. Religious commitment and mental health: a review of the empirical literature. J Psychol Theol 1991;19:6–25.
19 Comstock G, Partridge K. Church attendance and health. J Chronic Dis 1972;25:665–72.
20 Larson D., Wilson W. The religious life of alcoholics. Southern Medical Journal 1980;73:723–7.
21 Moore R, Mead L, Pearson T. Youthful precursors of alcohol abuse in physicians. Am J Med 1990;88:332–6.
22 Fraser G., Sharlik D. Risk factors for all–cause and coronary heart disease mortality in the oldest old: the Adventist's Health Study. Archives of Internal Medicine 1997;157(19):2249–58.
23 Levin J., Vanderpool H. Is frequent religious attendance really conducive to better health? Toward an epidemiology of religion. Soc Sci Med. 1987;24:589–600.
24 Kune G., Kune S., Watson L. Perceived religiousness is protective for colorectal cancer: data from the Melbourne Colorectal Cancer Study. Journal of the Royal Society of Medicine 1993;86:645–7.
25 Craigie F, Larson D, Liu I. References to religion in the Journal of Family Practice: dimensions and valency of spirituality. J Fam Pract 1990;30:477–80.
26 Hassed C. Western psychology meets Eastern philosophy. Australian Family Physician 1999;28(10):1057–8.
27 Hassed C. Spirituality and health. ANZAME Bulletin 2000;(1)27:5–6.
28 Astin J. Why patients use alternative medicine: results of a national study. JAMA 1998;279(19):1548–53.

HUMOUR: IS IT GOOD FOR YOU? p.76

1 Shammi P, Stuss D. Humour appreciation: a role of the right frontal lobe. Brain 1999;122(part 4):657–66.
2 Ozonoff S, Miller J. An exploration of right–hemisphere contributions to the pragmatic impairments of autism. 1996;52(3):411–34.
3 Shibles W. Feminism and the cognitive theory of emotion: anger, blame and humour. Women and Health 1991;17(1):57–69.
4 Abel M. Interaction of humour and gender in moderating relationships between stress and outcomes. Journal of Psychology 1998;132(3):267–76.
5 Berk L, Tan S, Fry W et al. Neuroendocrine and stress hormone changes during mirthful laughter. American Journal of Medical Science 1989;298:390–6.
6 Zautra A., Hoffman J., Potter P. et al. Examination of changes in interpersonal stress as a factor in disease exacerbations among women with rheumatoid arthritis. Annals of Behavioural Medicine. 1997;19(3):279–86.
7 Da Costa D., Dobkin P., Pinard L. et al. The role of stress in functional disability among women with systemic lupus erythematosis: a prospective study. Arthritis Care and Research. 1999;12(2):112–9.
8 Lehrer P. Emotionally triggered asthma: a review of research literature and some

hypotheses for self–regulation therapies. Applied Psychophysiology and Biofeedback 1998;23(1):13–41.

9 Strunk R, Mrazek D, Fuhrmann G et al. Physiologic and psychological characteristics associated with deaths due to asthma in childhood. A case controlled study. JAMA 1985;254(9):1193–8.

10 Anonymous. Internship: physicians respond to Norman Cousins. JAMA 1981;246(19):2141–4.

11 Elgee NJ. Norman Cousins' sick laughter redux. Archives of Internal Medicine 1990;150(8):1588.

12 Schipper H et al. A new biological framework for cancer research. Lancet 1996;348:1149.

13 Chrousos G The HPA axis and immune mediated inflammation. N Engl J Med 1995;332:1351.

14 Kearney R From theory to practice – The implications of the latest psychoneuroimmunology research and how to apply them. MIH Conference Proceedings 1998;171–88.

15 Dillon K, Totten M. Psychological factors, immunocompetence, and health of breast–feeding mothers and their infants. Journal of Genetic Psychology 1989;150(2):155–62.

16 Iribarren C, Sidney S, Bild D. et al. Association of hosility with coronary artery calcification in young adults. JAMA 2000;283(19):2546–51.

17 Yoder M, Haude R. Sense of humour and longevity: older adults' self–ratings compared with ratings for deceased siblings. Psychological Reports 1995;76(3 Pt1):945–6.

18 Gelkopf M, Kreitler S, Sigal M. Laughter in a spychiatric ward. Somatic, emotional, social, and clinical influences on schizophrenic patients. Journal of Nervous and Mental Disease 1993;181(5):283–9.

19 Harries G. Use of humour in patient care. British Journal of Nursing 1995;4(17):984–6.

20 Robbins J. Using humour to enhance learning in the skills laboratory. Nurse Educator 1994;19(3):39–41.

21 Abel M. Interaction of humour and gender in moderating relationships between stress and outcomes. Journal of Psychology 1998;132(3):267–76.

22 Moran C, Massam M. Differential influences of coping humour and humour bias on mood. Behavioural Medicine 1999;25(1):36–42.

23 Moran C. Short–term mood change, perceived funniness, and the effect of humour stimuli. Behavoural Medicine 1996;22(1):32–8.

24 Showalter S, Skobel S. American Journal of Hospice and Palliative Care 1996;13(4):8–9.

25 Saper B. The therapeutic use of humour for psychiatric disturbances of adolescents and adults. Psychiatric Quarterly 1990;61(4):261–72.

26 Perlini A, Nenonen R, Lind D. Effects of humour on test anxiety and performance. Psychological Reports 1999;84(3 part 2):1203–13.

27 Kurtz S. Humour as a perioperative nursing management tool. Seminars in perioperative Nursing 1999;8(2):80–4.

28 Beitz J. Keeping them in stitches: humour in perioperative education. Seminars in Perioperative Nursing 1999;8(2):71–9.

29 Vergeer G, MacRae A. Therapeutic use of humour in occupational therapy. Americal Journal of Occupational Therapy 1993;47(8):678–83.

30 Bain L. The place of humour in chronic or terminal illness. Professional Nurse 1997;12(10):713–5.
31 Savage L, Canody C. Life with a left ventricualr assist device: the patient's perspective. American Journal of Critical Care 1999;8(5):340–3.
32 Thorson J, Powell F. Sense of humour and dimensions of personality. Journal of Clinical Psychology 1993;49(6):799–809.
33 Hampes W. Relations between humour and generativity. Psychological Reports 1993;73(1):131–6.
34 Deaner S, McConatha J. The relation of humour to depression and personality. Psychological Reports 1993;72(3 Pt1):755–63.
35 Thorson J, Powell F, Sarmany–Schuller I et al. Psychological health and sense of humour. Journal of Clinical Psychology 1997;53(6):605–19.
36 Weisenberg M, Tepper I, Schwartzwald J. Humour as a cognitive technique for increasing pain tolerance. Pain 1995;63(2):207–12.
37 Weisenberg M, Raz T, Hener T. The influence of film–induced mood on pain perception. Pain 1998;76(3):365–75.
38 Matz A, Brown S. Humour and pain management. A review of current literature. Journal of Holistic Nursing 1998;16(1):68–75.
39 Prerost F. Presentation of humour and facilitation of a relaxatio response among internal and external scorers on Rotter's scale. Psychological Reports 1993;72(3 Pt2):1248–50.
40 Buchanan T, al'Absi M, Lovallo W. Cortisol fluctuates with increases and decreases in negative affect. Psychoneuroendocrinology 1999;24(2):227–41.
41 Lambert R, Lambert N. The effects of humour on secreatory immunoglobulin A levels in school–aged children. Pediatric Nursing 1995;21(1):16–9.
42 Berk L, Bittmen B, Covington T. et al. A video presentation of music, nature's imagery and positive affirmations as a combined eustress paradigm modulates neuroendocrine hormones. Annals of Behavioural Medicine 1997;19:201.
43 Berk L, Tan S, Fry W et al. Neuroendocrine and stress hormone changes during mirthful laughter. American Journal of Medical Science 1989;298:390–6.
44 Koh K. Emotion and immunity. Journal of Psychosomatic Research 1998;45(2):107–15.
45 Kamei T, Kumano H, Masumura S. Changes of immunoregulatory cells associated with psychological stress and humour. Perceptual and Motor Skills 1997;84(3 Pt2):1296–8.
46 Dillon K, Minchoff B, Baker K. Positive emotional states and enhancement of the immune system. International of Psychiatry in Medicine 1985;15:13–18.
47 Fry W. The physiological effects of humour, mirth and laughter. JAMA 1992;267(13):1857–8.

MEDICINE — WHAT HAS LOVE GOT TO DO WITH IT p.83

1. Marazziti D, Akiskal A, Rossi, et al. Alteration of platelet serotonin transporter in romantic love. Psychol Med 1999; 29:741–745.
2. Fisher H. Lust, attraction and attachment in mammalian reproduction. Hum Nat 1998; 9(1):23–52.
3. William Shakespeare. Sonnet No. 116.
4. Glassman A, Helzer J, Covey L, et al. Smoking, smoking cessation and major depression. JAMA 1990; 264:1546–1549.
5. Covey L, Glassman A, Stetner F, et al. Depression and depressive symptoms in smoking cessation. Compr Psychiatry 1990; 31:350–354.

6. Hall S, Munoz R, Reus V. Cognitive behavioural intervention increases abstinence rates for depressive history smokers. J Consult Clin Psychol 1994; 62:141–146.

7. Hurt R, Sachs D, Glover E, et al. A comparison of sustained–release bupropion and placebo for smoking cessation. N Engl J Med 1997; 337(17):1196–1202.

HEART AND SOUL p.87

1. Tennant C, McLean L. Mood disturbances and coronary heart disease: progress in the past decade. Med J Aust 2000; 172(4):151–152.

2. Hemingway H, Marmot M. Evidence based cardiology: psychosocial factors in the aetiology and prognosis of coronary heart disease. Br Med J 1999; 318(7196):1460–1467.

3. Rozanski A, Blumenthal J, Kaplan J. Impact of psychosocial factors on the pathogenesis of cardiovascular disease and implications for therapy. Circulation 1999; 99(16):2192–2217.

4. Linden W, Stossel C, Maurice J. Psychosocial interventions for patients with coronary artery disease: a meta analysis. Arch Int Med 1996; 156(7):745–752.

5. Moser D, Dracup K. Is anxiety early after myocardial infarction associated with subsequent ischaemic and arrhythmic events? Psychosom Med 1996; 58(5):395–401.

6. Kawachi I, Sparrow D, Voconas P, Weiss S. Symptoms of anxiety and risk of coronary heart disease. The Normative Aging Study. Circulation 1994; 90(5):2225–2229.

7. Kawachi I, Coditz G, Ascherio A, et al. Prospective study of phobic anxiety and risk of coronary heart disease in men. Circulation 1994; 89(5):1992–1997.

8. Kubzansky L, Kawachi I, Spiro A, et al. Is worrying bad for your heart? A prospective study of worry and coronary heart disease in the Normative Aging Study. Circulation 1997; 95(4):818–824.

9. Frasure–Smith N, Lesperance F, Talajic M. Depression and 18 month prognosis after myocardial infarction. Circulation 1995; 91(4):999–1005.

10. Appels A, Kop W, Bar F. Vital exhaustion, extent of atherosclerosis, and the clinical course after successful percutaneous transluminal coronary angioplasty. Eur Heart J 1995; 16(12):1880–1885.

11. Appels A, Otten F. Exhaustion as precursor of cardiac death. Br J Clin Psych 1992; 31(3):351–356.

12. Weissman M, Markowitz J, Ouellette R, et al. Panic disorder and cardiovascular/cerebrovascular problems: results from a community survey. Am J Psych 1990; 147(11):1504–1508.

13. Simonsick E, Wallace R, Blazer D, Berkman L. Depressive symptomatology and hypertension–associated morbidity and mortality in older adults. Psychosom Med 1995; 57(5):427–435.

14. Everson S, Kaplan G, Goldberg D, et al. Anger expression and incident stroke: prospective evidence from the Kuipio ischaemic heart disease study. Stroke 1999; 30(3):523–528.

15. Frasure–Smith N, Lesperance F, Prince R, et al. Randomised trial of home based psychosocial nursing intervention for patients recovering from myocardial infarction. Lancet 1997; 350(9076):473–479.

16. Jones D, West R. Psychological rehabilitation after myocardial infarction: multicentre randomised controlled trial. Br Med J 1996; 313:1517–1521.

17. Cohen H, Gibson G, Olderman M. Excess risk of myocardial infarction in patients treated with antidepressant medications; association with use of tricyclic agents. Am J Med 2000; 108:2–8.

CONNECTEDNESS — THE SOCIAL FACTOR AND HEALTH p.92
1. Miller M, Rahe R. Life changes scaling for the 1990's J Psychosom Res. 1997;43(3):279–292.
2. Cantor C, Neulinger K, De Leo D. Australian suicide trends 1964–1997: youth and beyond? MJA 1999; 171:137–141.
3. House J S, Landis K R, Umberson D. Social relationships and health. Science 1988: 241:540–545.
4. Lantz P M, House J S, Lepkowski J M et al. Socioeconomic factors, health behaviours, and mortality: results from a nationally representative prospective study of US adults. JAMA 1998; 279(21): 1703–1708.
5. Berkman L, Leo–Summers L, Horwitz R. Emotional support and survival after AMI: a prospective population–based study of the elderly. Ann Int Med 1992; 117:1003–1009.
6. Ruberman W, Weinblatt E, Goldberg J et al. Psychosocial influences on mortality after AMI. N Engl J Med 1984;311:552–559.
7. Leserman J, Jackson E, Petitto J, et al. Progression to AIDS: the effects of stress, depressive symptoms and social support. Psychosom Med 1999;61(3):397–406.
8. Resnick M D, Bearman P, Blum R, et al. Protecting adolescents from harm; findings from the National Longitudinal Study on Adolescent Health. JAMA 1997; 278(10):823–832.
9. Schattner P, Coman G. The stress of metropolitan general practice. MJA 1998;169(3):133–137.
10. McKelvey R, Davies L, Pfaff J, et al. Psychological distress and suicidal ideation among 15–24 year olds presenting to a general practice: a pilot study. Aust N Z J Psychiatry 1998;32(3)344–348.

MUSIC AS MEDICINE p.97
1. Marsilio Ficino. The letters of Marsilio Ficino. London: Shepheard–Walwyn 1975; 1:(letter 92).
2. Plato. The Republic.
3. Rauscher F, Shaw G, Lenine L, et al. Music training causes long term enhancement of preschool children's spatial–temporal reasoning. Neurol Res 1997; 19(l):2–8.
4. Rauscher F, Shaw G, Ky K. Listening to Mozart enhances spatial–temporal reasoning: towards a neurophysiologic basis. Neuroscience 1995; 185(l):44–47.
5. Mills B. Effects of music on assertive behaviour during exercise by middle school age students. Percept Mot Skills 1996; 83(2):423–426.
6. Robinson T, Weaver J, Zillman D. Exploring the relation between personality and the appreciation of rock music. Psychol Rep 1996; 78(l):259–269. 22.
7. McCraty R, Barrios–Choplin B, Atkinson M, et al. The effect of different types of music on mood, tension and mental clarity. Altern Ther Health Med 1998; 4(l):75–84.
8. Good M. Effects of relaxation and music on postoperative pain: a review. J Adv Nurs 1996; 24(5):905–914.
9. O'Callaghan C. Pain, music creativity and music therapy in palliative care. Am J Hosp Palliat Care 1996; 13(2):43–49.
10. Standley J, Hanser S. Music therapy research and applications in paediatric oncology treatment. J Pediatr Oncol Nurs 1995; 12(l):3–8.
11. Allen K, Blascovich J. Effects of music on cardiovascular reactivity among surgeons. JAMA 1994; 272(11):882–884.
12. Augustin P, Hains A. Effect of music on ambulatory surgery patient's preoperative anxiety. AORN J 1996; 63(4):750–758.
13. Krumhansi C. An exploratory study of musical emotions and psychophysiology. Can J Exp Psychol 1997; 51(4):336–353.
14. Kneafsey R. The therapeutic use of music in a care of the elderly setting: a literature review. J Clin Nurs 1997; 6(5):341–346.

15. Gardiner M, Fox A, Knowles F, et al. Learning improved by arts training. Nature 1996; 381(6580):284.
16. Hanser S, Thompson L. Effects of a music therapy strategy on depressed older adults. J Gerontol 1994; 49(6):265–269.
17. Chlan L. Psychophysiologic responses of mechanically ventilated patients of music: a pilot study. Am J Crit Care 1995; 4(3):233–238.
18. Guzzetta C. Effects of relaxation and music therapy on patients in a coronary care unit with presumptive acute myocardial infarction. Heart Lung 1989; 18(6):609–616.
19. Field T, Martinez A, Nawrocki T, et al. Music shifts frontal EEG in depressed adolescents. Adolescence 1998; 33(129):109–116.
20. Kabuto M, Nageyama T, Nitta H. EEG power spectrum changes due to listening to pleasant music and their relation to relaxation effects. Jpn J Hygiene 1993; 48(4):807–818.
21. Kalliopuska M, Ruokonen I. A study with a follow up of the effect of music education on holistic development of empathy. Percept Mot Skills 1993; 76(l):131–137.
22. Chametski C, Brennan F, Harrison J. Effect of music and auditory stimuli on secretory immunoglobulin A. Percept Mot Skills 1998; 87(3):1163–1170.

DO NO HARM p.101
1. Bhasale A, Miller G, Reid S, Britt H. Analysing potential harm in Australian general practice: an incident monitoring study. Med J Aust 1998; 169(2):73–76.
2. Wilson R, Runciman W, Gibbard R, et al. The quality in Australian health care study. Med J Aust 1995; 163:458–471.
3. Wilson R, Harrison B, Gibberd R, Hamilton J. An analysis of the causes of adverse events form the quality in Australian health care study. Med J Aust 1999; 170(9):411–415.
4. Health system costs of injury, poisoning and musculoskeletal disorders in Australia. Australian Institute of Health and Welfare, 1993–1994.
5. Romans–Clarkson S. Psychological sequelae of induced abortion. Aust N Z J Psych 1989; 23(4):555–565.
6. Ney P, Wickett A. Mental health and abortion: review and analysis. Psychiatr J Univ Ott 1989; 14(4):506–516.
7. Gissler M, et al. Suicides after pregnancy in Finland 1987–1994: register linkage study. Br Med J 1996; 313:1431–1434.
8. Thareaux–Deneux C, Bouyer J, Job–Spira N, et al. Risk of ectopic pregnancy and previous induced abortion. Am J Public Health 1998; 88(3):401–405.
9. Brind J, Chinchilli V, Severs W, et al. Induced abortion as an independent risk factor for breast cancer: a comprehensive review and meta–analysis. J Epidemiol Community Health 1996; 50(5):481–496.

TOWARDS A MORE ENLIGHTENED VIEW OF AUTONOMY P.111
1. Syme L. Mastering the control factor. The Health Report. ABC Radio. Health report transcript 9.11.1998. www.abc.net.au/rn.
2. Plato. The Republic. Translated by Benjamin Jowett. Great Books of the Western World. Book 4. Encyclopaedia Britannica.
3. Eysenck H, Grossarth-Maticek R. Creative novation behaviour therapy as a prophylactic treatment for cancer and coronary heart disease. Behav Res Ther 1991;29:1–31.
4. Grossarth-Maticek R, Eyseich H. Prophylactic effects of psychoanalysis on cancer prone and coronary heart disease prone probands, as compared with control groups and behaviour therapy groups. Behav Ther Exp Psychiatry 1990;21(2):91–99.

PATERNALISM — IS IT A PEJORATIVE TERM? p.114
1. Gillon R. Philosophical medical ethics. Wiley, 1991:67.

Index